Becoming

POLICE OFFICER

Becoming a
POLICE OFFICER

LEARNINGEXPRESS®

NEW YORK

Library of Congress Cataloging-in-Publication Data
Becoming a police officer.—1st ed.
   p. cm.
  Includes index.
  ISBN 978-1-57685-680-2
  1. Police—United States.   2. Law enforcement—United States.   I.
LearningExpress (Organization)
  HV8139.B43 2009
  363.20973—dc22

                                                    2009003121

Printed in the United States of America

9 8 7 6 5 4 3 2 1

First Edition

ISBN 978-1-57685-680-2

Regarding the Information in this Book

We attempt to verify the information presented in our books prior to publication. It is always a
good idea, however, to double-check such important information as minimum requirements,
application, and testing procedures and deadlines with the Department of Homeland Security
(DHS).

For more information or to place an order, contact LearningExpress at:

   2 Rector Street
   26th Floor
   New York, NY 10006

Or visit us at:
   www.learnatest.com

Contents

Introduction

ARE YOU the kind of person who enjoys helping others? Are you patient? Are you a good listener? Do you like working with people? Are you detail-oriented and able to multitask? Do you like a challenge? Are you able to keep your professional and personal lives separate? Would you like to help improve the lives of individuals and families? If so, then you might consider becoming a police officer.

Maybe you already know police officers working in the field and have some ideas about what a law enforcement career entails. Perhaps you don't know anyone in law enforcement at all. Whether you fall into the first category or the second, this book is for you. It is important to learn as much as you can about police work before making a career choice.

Becoming a Police Officer will allow you to widen your job search by describing the many types of law enforcement agencies. You will learn about law enforcement careers you might not have considered yet. Keep in mind that there are almost 18,000 police agencies in the United States—more than anyplace else in the world. And they can range in size from a single officer to approximately 38,000!

Where do you fit in? What should you be doing right now to prepare yourself for a career in policing? *Becoming a Police Officer* will not only show you the many roles a police officer can play, but it will also help you decide whether policing is the career for you. Its goal is to prepare you for the process of becoming a police officer. This book will help you become one of the nearly 5 million men and women who have served as police officers since the nation's founding and, more importantly, one of the approximately 750,000 people currently serving.

HOW TO USE THIS BOOK

To get the most out of *Becoming a Police Officer*, be sure to read each chapter carefully.

As you do this, consider the minimum requirements for most police positions. Think about the many types of agencies that exist and whether some are more appropriate for you than others. Should you consider an agency that requires you to live away from home for your initial training? Does an agency with policies that call for frequent travel or transfers meet your or your family's needs? Are there types of agencies in your area that you never knew about or never considered as part of your job search that now sound very appealing to you?

In addition, reflect on your educational goals. Should you enroll in a college-level police studies or criminal justice program? If so, should it be a two-year or four-year institution? Are there ways to get help paying for your education?

Becoming a Police Officer will answer these questions and many others that may come up as you learn more about this career. Always keep your personal goals in mind and use the information in this book to help achieve them.

Becoming a

POLICE OFFICER

CHAPTER one

THE HISTORY OF POLICING

*When I joined my local municipal police department in 1983, I was a
"people-oriented" young woman who wanted a non-traditional career.
Although I was the first woman on my department and found myself
challenged daily by both co-workers and the public, I have never
doubted that I made the right choice. I look back in pride at the people I
was able to help over my twenty-five years of service. . . . I enjoyed the
challenge of problem solving in my roles of patrol officer, detective, and
supervisor. . . . Police work isn't for everyone, but it is a career that can
provide personal satisfaction because you have the power to actually
make a difference in people's lives—often for the better.*

—Retired police officer, 25 years of experience

WHEN PEOPLE say they want to be police officers they often have a certain set of images in mind. Generally, they think of either patrol or detective work. To most people, the first involves patrolling in uniform in a marked patrol car, looking for and catching criminals. The second, depicted in countless movies and television dramas, involves working in street clothes and responding to crimes after they have occurred, interviewing witnesses, arresting a suspect and working with the prosecutor's office to prepare for trial, testify, and be there when the jury announces a guilty verdict. If only the job of a police officer was actually as simple as it's depicted in films and on television!

For many people hoping to become police officers, the thought of an exciting career plays a large role in their decision. Police departments know this. Although they often try to discourage applicants who are action junkies, they also contribute to this viewpoint. In urging candidates to consider the New York City Police Department (NYPD) immediately after annual salaries were raised about $10,000, the department's ad in a local newspaper stressed not money but "an adventure waiting to happen." Some police officers even refer to their jobs as a front seat to the greatest show on earth.

JUST THE FACTS

The word *police* comes from the Latin word *politia* or from the Greek word *politiea*, each of which can be translated to mean *civil administration*.

Of course, neither of these descriptions fits what can be long hours of driving or walking around when nothing happens, of issuing traffic tickets to people who would like you to disappear, of hearing stories that sound like fairy tales, or of knowing that people may die in your arms. But there is also the satisfaction of being able to help a sick or disoriented person, deliver a baby, or somehow save the day for someone in danger.

Will any or all of these things happen in the course of a day? A week? A month? A year? A whole career? The answer may depend on you, on where you police, and a little bit of luck.

Police officers fulfill so many different roles in so many different agencies. The major categories of police agencies include local police; county police; county sheriffs' offices; state police; and special jurisdiction police, which might include airports, parks, transit systems, and federal law enforcement agencies. There are also parts of the country where city or county prosecutors employ their own investigators. Other city, county, or state agencies with investigative powers may also hire and train their own personnel to investigate areas such as Medicare or Medicaid fraud, violation of liquor or other licensing requirements, or allegations of child or elder abuse, to name just a few.

Policing, especially in the United States, is a fragmented field. There are about 18,000 agencies defined as police departments, with employees who are authorized by law to make arrests and use force. This number does not include the many investigative agencies whose employees have limited arrest authority and may lack the authority to carry firearms.

JUST THE FACTS

Some of the earliest records of policing are from the Middle East, where ruling regimes in Mesopotamia set up policelike agencies more than 6,000 years ago. A police force separate from the military existed in Egypt in around 2000 B.C.E. Despite these very early forms of policing, the first organization that would be recognizable today as police were the Roman *vigiles* created around 27 B.C.E. It is from the vigiles that we get the word *vigilantes*, which today conjures up images of an unruly mob rather than of peacekeepers. It is also the root from which we get the concept of vigilance, or watchfulness, the basis of early watch and ward societies and committees on vigilance that predated police departments in many cities and towns. The number of vigiles must have been vast; more than 9,000 were included in what is probably the first special unit of police, the Praetorian Guard, who were assigned to protect their founder, Augustus Caesar (Emperor Augustus).

THE SHERIFF'S OFFICE

Sheriff departments are the nation's oldest law enforcement agencies. In the United States, sheriffs are generally county administrators with both civil and criminal responsibilities. (In Lousiana, they are called "parish administrators.") Their civil responsibilities can be seen in their roles as tax collectors, enforcers of non-criminal legal judgments, and in their responsibilities for conducting sheriffs' auctions, events at which properties with tax liens are sold so that the back taxes can be paid and the properties returned to the tax rolls. Stemming from their judicial roots, modern sheriffs are officers of the court who provide court security and protection of judges and prosecutors and who fulfill their custodial role by operating the county jail.

Over time, some sheriffs' offices, particularly in larger counties where there is a county police force or where there are numerous municipal police departments with adjacent jurisdictions, have shed their policing roles and have only court, jail, and civil responsibilities. In these departments, deputy sheriffs—the rank in a sheriff's office that is the equivalent of police officer— do not patrol at all.

JUST THE FACTS

The office of sheriff was well-established in the parts of colonial North America that were under British rule. The earliest sheriffs, as in Great Britain, were appointed by the crown, but immediately upon the states declaring independence in 1776, Maryland began to elect sheriffs, setting a pattern that would continue through much of the nation until the present time.

Today, only Alaska, Connecticut, and Hawaii do not appoint or elect sheriffs. In the other 47 states, the vast majority of the slightly more than 3,000 sheriffs continue to be elected officials. As of 2008, sheriffs were elected for four-year terms in forty-one states, two-year terms in three states, a three-year term in one state, and a six-year term in one state. Sheriffs are usually considered the chief law enforcement officers of their counties and are generally deferred to by local police chiefs. This is particularly true in rural counties, where the police departments are generally smaller than the sheriff's office and the local police depend on the sheriff's office for assistance in all but routine patrol matters. In some states, there are laws which specify how many terms a sheriff may serve. These term limits were developed primarily because voters and state-level politicians were often concerned about how powerful a sheriff could become by enforcing both civil and criminal law.

JUST THE FACTS

The constable is a law enforcement role that has fallen into disuse in much of the United States but is still found in the south and parts of the west, especially throughout Texas.

The histories of many police departments often describe the first officers as having been constables.

The first constables in what would become the United States were often unpaid and untrained elected officials who oversaw the night watch, administered punishments, and also were expected to provide a minimum level of safety for citizens during daylight hours. The title of constable evolved into an office that came to be called the town marshal, often shortened to the one-word title of marshal.

LOCAL POLICE DEPARTMENTS

Local policing in the United States is generally associated with attempts by a few large eastern cities, primarily Boston, New York, and Philadelphia, to establish departments modeled after the London Metropolitan Police, a force established in 1829 in England by Sir Robert Peel.

What we would today recognize as police departments began to develop in the mid-1830s, when industrialization, urbanization, and the arrival of immigrants led to previously unseen levels of civil disorder throughout much of the nation, in cities as well as small towns. These changes led the largest cities, including Philadelphia in 1833, Boston in 1838, and New York in 1845, to combine their day and night watches into 24-hour paid police departments. Due to organizational issues, New York City's police department is often considered the first fully paid, professional 24-hour police department. Each, though, was an attempt to copy Peel's model and is recognized today as a forerunner of modern police departments, defined as those employing full-time officers who are primarily involved in patroling defined areas (generally termed *beats*) for the purpose of preventing crime.

By the 1880s, members of most police departments were armed, and in urban areas they were uniformed. Regulations for hiring and promotion brought some stability to police employment. Also around this time, departments placed more emphasis on officers patrolling in uniform so they would be visible to both citizens and supervisors. As small communities grew into towns and then into cities, they went from a small number of constables and town marshals to a 24-hour local police department, often augmented by the sheriff's office.

This patchwork nature of policing is so woven into law enforcement that it is difficult even to cite the number of departments. The generally-agreed-to figure of about 18,000 policing agencies in the United States represents all agencies, including municipal, county, state, federal, campus, and other special jurisdiction departments. Of this total, about 13,000 are municipal (village, town, or city) or county police agencies; about 3,000 are sheriffs' offices, and 49 are state police agencies. In addition, there are about 1,500 special jurisdiction police agencies and about 500 constable jurisdictions.

COUNTY POLICE DEPARTMENTS

County police departments are different from county sheriffs' offices. They are closer in organization and development to local police. County police departments, beginning in 1925 in Nassau County, NY, developed primarily in counties surrounding large cities that saw population and traffic increases. These increases often overwhelmed the small, fragmented agencies that policed the small communities, leading to mergers and eventually to county police forces. County police departments still tend to be located around large metropolitan areas. Among the largest are the Nassau and Suffolk county departments east of New York City; the Prince Georges and Montgomery county departments in Maryland, and the Arlington and Fairfax county departments in Virginia.

STATE POLICE AGENCIES

Most state police agencies were formed later than sheriffs' offices and local police departments. For that reason they have concurrent (or shared) jurisdiction or responsibility with these agencies. The earliest state police department organized similarly to today's agencies did not appear until 1903 in Connecticut.

The Texas Rangers were formed in 1835, when Texas gained independence from Mexico. The Rangers, who are still in existence, could not consider themselves a state police agency until 1845, when Texas, which had been a republic, became the 28th state in the union.

Arizona and New Mexico formed mounted patrol agencies prior to statehood, in 1901 and 1905, respectively. Both also became state police agencies when those territories became states about a month apart in 1912. The roles of the Texas, Arizona, and New Mexico units, though, were unlike those of modern state police agencies. While they did have certain investigative responsibilities, their primary tasks involved patroling the border with Mexico, making them more like today's U.S. Border Patrol than a state police agency.

The original Connecticut State Police would be unrecognizable today. The agency was developed for the narrow role of combating the growth of illegal liquor markets throughout the state. Without vehicles, the original five troopers rode the state's railroads to investigate reports of illegal manufacture, transport, and sales of liquor. Lacking their own communications network, they relied on shopkeepers to set up a relay system between the commander and officers in the field. Even earlier, in 1865, Massachusetts had also formed a state police force specifically to combat the failure of local police to enforce laws against alcohol trafficking. Controversy plagued the force; it was disbanded in 1875 and once re-established remained fairly small until 1925, when it grew to 50 officers who were stationed in barracks across the state. Because of the early history of the Massachusetts State Police, the Connecticut State Police claim to be the first state police agency. The Massachusetts State Police dispute that claim.

The most active years of state police department development were between 1917 and the 1930s. Their origins are often attributed to the new-found mobility of criminals due to the development of the automobile. In fact, creation of state police agencies was often a battleground between urban and rural politicians and between advocates of labor, who saw state police as primarily strike-breaking forces, and business elites, who cited the inability of local police and sheriffs' offices to curtail local crime. Some elected officials were also concerned about the costs of creating statewide police agencies, but saw them as answers to what were thought to be the inadequacies of sheriffs' officers and small, rural police departments to address growing concerns with crime in the years after World War I.

For these reasons, as a political compromise, a number of state police agencies were originally limited to highway enforcement. Some of these eventually expanded their jurisdictions to become full-service agencies; others did not and remained highway patrol forces.

Today all 50 states with the exception of Hawaii have some type of state police agency, but not all state police agencies are alike. Some are categorized as full-service agencies with multiple law enforcement roles and others are primarily highway patrol agencies. Many state police agencies tend to be more highly centralized agencies than municipal, county, or sheriffs' departments, and they operate in a manner more closely resembling military discipline and demeanor than other police organizations. As part of this ethos, state police tend to put a greater emphasis on physical agility and ability. Not only are candidates faced with arduous physical standards for entry and for graduation from the academy, but in many agencies officers are tested annually to assure they remain in peak physical conditions.

FEDERAL LAW ENFORCEMENT

Unlike most other countries, the United States does not maintain a national police force. This may come as a surprise to many, who believe that the Federal Bureau of Investigation (FBI) fulfills that role. Although the FBI may be the best-known federal law enforcement agency, it shares jurisdiction with many agencies, the majority of which are much older than the FBI. Federal law enforcement, like the other areas of U.S. policing, is also fragmented.

A number of the earliest federal law enforcement agencies trace their histories to the colonial period, therefore predating the federal government itself. Among these are the Customs Service (now ICE), the Coast Guard, the Postal Inspection Service (PIS), and the Marshals Service.

Early federal law enforcers were assigned specific duties; this was because each agency was itself mission-specific. None were general purpose agencies similar to municipal police departments and, to a lesser extent, sheriffs' offices. Generally, the missions revolved around enforcing tax and tariff laws. The agencies were designed to enforce law violations that deprived either the government of funds or citizens of the few services for which they depended on the federal government. Thus, the Revenue Cutter Service, the forerunner of today's Coast Guard, was created in 1789 to address the problems of smuggling. The mission of its collectors, each of whom oversaw a port district, was to collect duties (taxes) owed the government. The duties were based on the weight of the ships coming into the ports or on the merchandise carried on the ships. Because the job involved collection of monies, it was placed in the cabinet-level Department of the Treasury under the authority of the Secretary of the Treasury.

This set the tone for the decentralization of federal law enforcement. The Marshals Service was also created in 1789; its mission was to provide law enforcement personnel to support the work of the fledgling federal court system. The Marshals had a particularly high profile in the developing western part of the nation, where they were called on to provide law enforcement services in areas with few organized police departments. In the late 19th and early 20th century, in Indian Territory (now the state of Oklahoma), and later in the territories of Alaska and Hawaii, U.S. Marshals were for many years the only symbols of federal control, much like the Royal Canadian Mounted Police (RCMP) were in western Canada. In keeping with its history, the Marshals Service today, in addition to providing security at federal courts, and to administering the witness protection program, houses federal detainees and searches for federal fugitives.

Even earlier, the U.S. Post Office created a force of surveyors to attack the problems of mail theft. Although the current title postal inspector was not created until 1836, the Postal Inspection Service (PIS) traces its history to 1772, when Postmaster General Benjamin Franklin appointed surveyors to regulate and audit postal functions. The title was changed to special agent in 1801; in 1830 the tasks were centralized, even though the agents themselves were scattered around the country.

Initially concerned mostly with internal theft of the mails, this focus began to change in the 1850s when, as the mail moved west, mail thefts from ships, stagecoaches, and the railroads increased. Train robberies became more common after the Civil War; since a major target of train robbers was the U.S. mail, which at the time often contained cash and valuable goods, postal inspectors were assigned to many of these cases. As with many agencies, the PIS changed as criminal activity changed; beginning in the 1920s agents investigated a large number of fake lotteries, fraudulent advertising in newspapers and magazines carried through the mail, and birth control advocates who advertised or sent their products through the mail. Today, any crimes that involve the Post Office are investigated by postal inspectors. The crimes include mailing fraudulent documents and illegal substances, sending threats through the mail, commiting identity fraud, which often begins with stolen mail, and destroying of a public mailbox or other postal facility.

Indicating the broad range of federal law enforcement, another early force is one of the largest of the federal uniformed agencies. The U.S. Capitol Police (USCP) traces its origins to the appointment in 1801 of a watchman. Although he had only citizen's arrest powers, he was expected to protect the new seat of government when it moved from Philadelphia to Washington, DC. After experimenting with having U.S. Marines supplement the watchman service, in 1852 the Capitol Police was created. It was comprised of a chief, four assistant police officers, and two individuals who patrolled the grounds. From these fairly humble beginnings, the USCP has grown to a force of more than 1,000 officers. They are responsible for almost 200 acres of federal property, and also protect members and officers of Congress and their families. It is one of a number of all- or primarily uniformed police departments maintained by the federal government.

The Secret Service, established in 1865, was designated to investigate and prosecute counterfeiting of U.S. currency and, like the Coast Guard, was located in the Department of the Treasury. In the years after the Civil War, counterfeiting was rampant and the government found itself in need of vast amounts of money to support efforts to rebind the nation. At the time, it was estimated that as much as one-third of the nation's currency was counterfeit. The role of protecting the president was not added to Secret Service duties until 1901; today Secret Service agents are also assigned to protect the vice president, former presidents and their families, and candidates for president and vice president and their families.

Until it was overshadowed by the FBI, the Secret Service was the nation's leading general investigative agency; its members, termed operatives before the phrase special agent came into use, were often lent to other federal departments to assist in investigating complex crimes.

In part due to turf battles between the Department of the Treasury and the Department of Justice and in part to curtail the borrowing of Secret Service agents, in 1908 the DOJ created its own investigative agency, the

Bureau of Investigation (BOI). Its agents lacked power; most were unarmed and few were held in high regard. After a series of scandals involving the BOI, J. Edgar Hoover was named director in 1924, a position he held until 1972, one of the longest tenures in U.S. government history. Renamed the FBI in 1935, Hoover moved from chasing alleged subversives (mostly Communists) to chasing bank robbers and car thieves. Although never a local police officer, he was able to position himself for decades as a spokesman for U.S. policing. Through use of the media and a talent for consolidating power, he was also instrumental in turning the FBI into one of the most recognized law enforcement agencies in the world, the topic of countless books, movies, and television shows and the one most often mentioned as their choice of employment by candidates who aspire to federal law enforcement careers.

SPECIAL JURISDICTION POLICE AGENCIES

In its 2004 census of state and local police agencies, the DOJ's Bureau of Justice Statistics (BJS) found that more than 1,500 state and local police agencies served special geographic areas or had special enforcement or investigative agencies. Despite a wide range of jurisdictions and sizes, these agencies are generally termed special jurisdiction police agencies. While many of the individual agencies are not as large as county or state police departments or large municipal police departments, together they employ more than 85,000 people, about 50,000 of whom are sworn police officers. Although there are a number of ways of grouping these agencies, BJS has chosen to group them into five categories, specifically public buildings and facilities, natural resources and parks and recreation, transportation systems and facilities, criminal investigations, and special enforcement.

Each of these groups of agencies has a very different history, although many share in common having started as security departments, often employing retired local police officers. The largest single category of special enforcement police is represented by about 500 campus police departments serving four-year public institutions, which employ more than 10,000 officers. Two-year colleges and public school districts employed approximately 5,000 additional officers.

Another large segment is comprised of transportation-related police. These agencies cover airports, mass transit systems and railroads, ports, bridges and tunnels, and a small number of multipurpose or miscellaneous agencies; they employ about 9,000 additional officers, somewhat less than the more than 14,000 employed in the category of natural resources, parks and recreation.

WOMEN IN POLICING

Women began working in jails and prisons as early as the 1820s and as sheriffs' deputies and matrons as early as the 1880s. However, their official recognition generally is considered to be 1910 when Alice Stebbins Wells was hired by the Los Angeles Police Department (LAPD) and became the first woman with the unique title of policewoman. Not only was the title different from men's titles, the job responsibilities were very different from men's duties and with few exceptions defined the roles of women in policing until the 1960s and 1970s when federal laws and court challenges by women brought the right to equal employment in policing.

Wells was part of the generation of the first women to attend college. She was part of a larger movement in the late nineteenth and early twentieth century of women into full-time employment outside the home, generally in fields where they sought to help other women, often those poorer and less educated than they were. Most of these policewomen had been social workers or were involved in religious activities. They were concerned with what they saw as increasing immorality, juvenile delinquency, and alcohol consumption among the lower classes.

By the 1920s and 1930s a number of cities with large African-American populations appointed a very small number of black policewomen specifically to work with women and girls in the African-American community. Although these policewomen were not all college graduates, much like their white colleagues they were often members of the upper strata of society, including a number who were wives of pastors or leaders in their community.

In municipal policing women's promotional opportunities were often severely limited until the 1950s and 1960s. During this time period, a few women brought lawsuits to ensure the right to take tests for the rank of sergeant. Even after winning these suits, many were forced, as in New York City, to sue a second time for the right to become lieutenants.

Small departments, if they had women at all, employed one or two, often combining the jobs of matron and policewoman. In the largest departments, quotas for women were capped at no more than 1% of total staff. Women worked primarily in women's bureaus, often located away from a station-house and often sharing facilities with juvenile justice or corrections staffs.

Opportunities in state policing were virtually nonexistent. With the exception of the Connecticut and Massachusetts state police, each of which employed a handful of policewomen, no women were employed in state policing until the early 1970s.

Women's roles in municipal policing and sheriff's offices began to change officially in 1968. It was not until the mid-1970s, though, that women began to be hired according to the same standards applied to men (previously, standards have been higher, including in many cases a college degree or social work experience; height, weight, and physical agility standards were also quite different) and to receive academy training along with their male colleagues. The impetus for the change was passage in 1972 of Title VII of the 1964 Civil Rights Act, which extended to police agencies earlier prohibitions against employment discrimination on the basis of sex.

An additional push for legal equality was passage in 1973 of the Crime Control Act, which specified that agencies guilty of discrimination would not receive federal funds. With the possible loss of federal money, departments began to take seriously the requirement to hire women. By the end of the decade the titles of policewoman and policeman (or patrolman) were replaced in most agencies by the unisex title of police officer.

Prior to 1971, with the exception of the Marshals Service, which has employed women throughout its history, virtually no women had worked as special agents. Change came slowly; in 1969, President Richard M. Nixon issued Executive Order 11478, which prohibited discrimination in federal employment because of race, color, religion, sex, national origin, handicap, or age. It followed on the heels of Executive Order 11375, signed by President Lyndon B. Johnson in 1967, which had added sex to the existing prohibited forms of discrimination (race, color, religion, and national origin). But earlier regulations that barred women from jobs that required carrying a firearm kept them from special agent positions until 1971, when the Secret Service and the Postal Inspection Service became the first agencies to swear in women. The FBI and many other agencies followed in 1973.

Although women continue to be employed in all branches of law enforcement in considerably smaller numbers and percentages than men, legal equality has been achieved.

MINORITY MEN IN POLICING

Most of the history of minorities in American policing is based on the experiences of women and African-Americans; comparatively little has been written about Hispanic-Americans or Asian-Americans. The histories of African-American men and of women are similar in some key areas; both were hired primarily to police their own group and both were for much of their histories segregated within their departments.

Like women, black male police officers needed higher qualifications than white men did. Some of the earliest black officers were college graduates, but, like women, were not permitted to advance beyond the rank of police officer and were rarely considered for specialist assignments unless their race was viewed as helpful for particular types of cases.

A major difference between early policewomen and African-American men, though, is that the women sought segregation from the male police hierarchy while African-American men had this forced on them, even in parts of the country where segregation of the races was not legally imposed.

Free men of color served on the New Orleans, LA, city guard and constabulary as early as 1803 and were appointed to the New Orleans Gendarmerie in 1805; blacks would serve until 1830. New Orleans has always been a multiracial city, and these men's service was something of an oddity, although their role of policing other freed blacks or slaves was typical of the police tasks that were open to blacks. Also typical, their positions were based on political ebb and flow. Although the history of American policing is closely tied to local political shifts, minority men and all women were particularly likely to be employed only when local politicians saw a need for their services and to be dismissed during changes in local administration or during times of fiscal constraint.

By the time an African-American again joined the New Orleans Police Department in 1867, after the Civil War, other southern cities that had added newly enfranchised black citizens to government positions also added them to their police departments. Northern and Midwestern departments that employed black police officers prior to 1900 included Chicago; Pittsburgh, PA; Indianapolis, IN; Boston; Cleveland; Philadelphia; Columbus, OH; Los Angeles; Cincinnati, OH; Detroit; Brooklyn, NY (prior to its consolidation into New York City), and St. Louis, MO. New York City did not employ its first post-consolidation African-American officer until 1911. In the majority of these cities, blacks were not permitted to arrest white citizens and were discouraged from having any contact at all with white people. Their assignments were virtually always to police the black areas of their cities. To assure that no white citizens took offense at power having been granted to them, the black police officers rarely were permitted to work in uniform, since this would be seen as a sign of status having been granted to them by the municipality. Black police officers were also rarely granted promotional opportunities. Even when a very few, starting in Boston in 1895 and Chicago in 1897, were permitted to become sergeants, they continued to work in plainclothes and to supervise only black officers working in black areas.

Despite these limitations, blacks in the post–Civil War Reconstruction south achieved higher enrollment percentages on some police departments than today, including 50% in both Montgomery, AL, and Vicksburg, MS; 42% in Charleston, SC; 37% in Mobile, AL, and more than 25% in New Orleans and Portsmouth, VA. Most of these gains were erased by the 1880s, when patterns of pre–Civil War segregation returned. By 1880, only Memphis, which had had no black police in 1870, had a force that was more than 20% African-American. Continuing to undo Civil War-era changes in society, by the 1890s most southern cities had removed all or most African-Americans from their departments. Beginning in the 1950s, African-Americans were able to increase their percentages of police jobs somewhat, although those percentages remained in the single digits.

In the north, blacks, like women, continued to be appointed often outside the civil service system. In cities where there was a sizable African-American population that wielded local political power, politicians encouraged police chiefs to appoint black officers. Again, as with policewomen, many small cities decided that one black policeman was sufficient to respond to political pressures for their appointments and to provide police services to their group.

Black men, like women, were segregated. Often they were in bureaus that were located within African-American neighborhoods and were discouraged from leaving the confines of those areas. A study conducted in the 1950s found that more than half of the 130 cities and counties in the south that employed black police officers required them to call white officers if a white person was to be arrested. In many communities at this time, the police cars in which African-American officers patrolled were marked differently from the cars white officers used. Even in areas that are today culturally diverse, such as Miami, FL, until the 1950s there were separate promotion tests and lists for black and white police officers. There continued to be black police beats in many cities throughout the nation until the 1960s. The Miami Police Department even maintained an African-American police station until 1963.

Again similar to the barriers that stalled the careers of women, many departments did not permit black officers to vie for promotions. The few who were promoted were often relegated to assignments in which they would not supervise white officers. They were rarely permitted to exercise supervisory responsibility over any but the few black officers below them in rank. Reflecting residential patterns, political power, and the vestiges of segregation, two Ohio cities (Portsmouth and Cleveland) had appointed black police chiefs in 1962 and 1970, respectively, before Charleston, SC, and Houston in 1971 and 1974 respectively had promoted their first black sergeants.

Despite their limited roles in policing, it is important to remember that when women and black lawmen were first granted arrest authority it was years before they were granted the vote and, in the case of African-Americans, well before they were granted citizenship. What had originally, though, seemed like a great advance in their positions, came eventually to represent segregation that each group was forced to overcome to achieve legal equality in policing.

African-American men have had a longer history in federal law enforcement than women. Bass Reeves, a slave who escaped to Indian Territory after a fight that resulted in his beating his master, was appointed the first black deputy marshal west of the Mississippi River in 1875. He did not retire until 1907, when he was 83 years old. Other African-Americans also served as deputy U.S. marshals, primarily in the western portion of the country. Frederick Douglass, the abolitionist leader who served as an advisor to President Abraham Lincoln during the Civil War, was named the first African-American U.S. Marshal by President Rutherford Hayes in 1877.

The histories of the participation of other minority groups in policing are less likely to have been formally recorded. Most of what is known has been learned from local agency histories or from the fraternal associations representing the various groups. Because much of the southwestern United States was once a part of Mexico and Latinos continued to exercise political power in the pre-statehood and early-statehood periods, many of the early sheriffs in the areas that became the states of New Mexico and Arizona were Latino. Many were elected to multiple two-year terms; in San Miguel County, NM, the Romero family controlled the sheriff's office for decades prior to statehood. Similarly, Elfego Baca, born during the Civil War, was a deputy sheriff in Socorro County, NM, who eventually became an attorney, a deputy U.S. marshal, the mayor of Socorro, and, in 1919, the elected sheriff of Socorro County.

The records of the National Law Enforcement Officers Memorial Fund (NLEOMF), which records the histories of officers killed in the line of duty has identified a deputy sheriff killed in a gunfight in Monterey County, CA, in 1855 as the first Hispanic officer to be killed in the line of duty. The San Diego, CA, Police Department (SDPD) hired a former deputy marshal as its first Hispanic officer in the early 1890s.

The history of Asian-Americans is even more difficult to trace. Once again, it often requires reviewing the histories of individual police departments, many of which, particularly since the 1970s and 1980s, have sought to reassure applicants of different ethnicities that they are welcome within the ranks by highlighting the presence of similar officers in earlier decades. By 1917, for instance, the SDPD listed Chinese-American officers within its ranks.

Minority groups have increased their presence in policing since the 1970s, primarily through legislation and court cases. The Equal Employment Opportunities Act of 1972 extended the provisions of the Civil Rights Act of 1964, including Title VII, to state and local governments. Title VII of the original 1964 act had prohibited job discrimination based on race, color, religion, sex, or national origin. Many minority groups were also unable to gain large numbers of police positions because of various civil service entry requirements, especially those pertaining to height.

A Supreme Court decision that had nothing to do with policing ended many of these requirements. In the case of *Griggs v. Duke Power Company* (401 U.S. 424), the Court ruled in 1971 that hiring standards that could not be shown to be job-related and that discriminated against certain groups were unconstitutional and that it was the obligation of the employer to show that the selection standards were relevant. Police departments were unable to show the relevancy of many of their height and weight requirements. Some of the specific physical agility tests were also determined to have no relevance to tasks police officers were expected to perform. While certainly not all Asians or Hispanics are shorter than white men, the restrictions limiting police employment to those at least 5'7", and for state policing often 5'9", that had reduced their numbers were discarded, leading to their greater presence in policing today. Today, regardless of your size, sex, or ethnicity, if you are able to meet height/weight proportionality requirements and the other requirements explained in Chapter 2 you stand an excellent chance of fulfilling your interest in a police career.

CHAPTER two

BECOMING A POLICE OFFICER

I have made more moves than most throughout my career. I began as a corrections officer and after finishing college in New York, my hometown, I moved to Georgia to join a county police department. After Sept. 11, 2001, my career path moved into the areas of homeland security and emergency management. A new chief at a transit agency brought me in to command an emergency preparedness unit. I believe that my work constitutes twenty-first century policing strategies in combating high-tech crimes, global terror threats, and various disasters. Policing is becoming more specialized and integrated with state and federal partners in addition to traditional responsibilities. It is a great time to consider a career in law enforcement because of these opportunities and interesting fields of specialization.

—Sergeant in a special jurisdiction police agency

THE CURRENT job outlook for police officers is excellent; in fact, many police agencies throughout the United States have reported problems filling available vacancies.

For the past several years, many cities have offered signing bonuses to new officers and have paid incumbent officers a cash premium for each officer they recommended who completed the police academy. Departments have advertised in newspapers and on billboards in cities across the nation to attract candidates to their departments. An example of how far away from home some departments will roam occurred in summer 2008, when the Seattle Police Department placed ads outside New York City subway stations to attract candidates, much to the dismay of the New York City Police Department. Many departments also travel to college campuses not only to recruit, but to actually administer the entry test to interested students.

Many reasons have been suggested for the large number of vacancies but none seem to provide satisfactory answers. Many police leaders believe that young people today are less interested in careers that pay rewards over a long period of time and that, due in part to the influence of the Internet and the need for instant gratification, they are unwilling to go through the long and cumbersome process required to become police officers. Others have pointed to what they see as a general decline in good heath among young adults, who medical professionals have claimed are less healthy than earlier generations because of sedentary activities that have led to record-high levels of obesity and diabetes.

Still others point to the long-term affects of discontinuing the military draft, since veterans have historically made up a large portion of police recruits. Additional observers point to the increasing numbers of young people attending college; others decry the absence of discipline in society, resulting in young people being unwilling to spend their careers in organizations where they must often work nights and weekends, and generally face demands on their personal time and lifestyles. Each of these so-called theories raises as many questions as it claims to answer.

The need for new police officers is also influenced by the number of officers retiring. At a time when government budgets may no longer be increasing and when monies provided for homeland security may also diminish, some agencies will be primarily filling positions that currently exist as officers retire. Historically agencies have hired in periods when crime was high or funding was available. Many police agencies grew in the 1960s in response to concerns about crime and a national political focus on the issue. Because most police agencies allow officers to retire on full pension after 20 or 25 years, hiring tends to be cyclical. Those who were hired in the late 1960s and early 1970s retired by the 1990s, and now many of the officers who replaced them are preparing to retire, creating a new cycle of hiring.

Additionally, many agencies have added to their staffs to accommodate community policing styles, which tend to be more labor-intensive than traditional motor patrol. Others have increased their responsibilities in homeland-security-related areas, which have caused additional hiring. The creation of the federal Department of Homeland Security (DHS) has opened many new federal law enforcement jobs as older agencies, including the FBI, have been given new mandates that call for hiring special agents with never-before-required skills. The focus on homeland security has also affected state and local policing. Many agencies have taken on new responsibilities that have stretched their staffs and have created demands for greater specialization, including working with canines, bomb detection, and various investigative areas.

Each of these growing areas of employment makes for an excellent job outlook for police candidates.

EARNINGS AND BENEFITS FOR POLICE OFFICERS

Most candidates for law enforcement jobs are idealists. Studies over the past few decades that have asked those attending a police academy why they are becoming police officers always discover that the primary reason is to help others. Some candidates are looking for job satisfaction. Others are looking for a job that provides adventure, one in which they will be outdoors, and can expect the opportunity to make independent judgments (termed *exercising discretion*) in policing. Since most know they will need to work for most of their adult lives, the substantial salary and fringe benefits of a police career are generally also mentioned among the top four or five reasons.

Before taking a job in any field, you will need to decide on your own salary requirements. Do you live in a big city and plan to stay there? Are you willing to relocate to a less expensive suburb or rural area? Do you have a family to support? Are you paying off student loans? No matter how much you enjoy your work, your job will need to meet your salary requirements in order for you to stay with it.

JUST THE FACTS

Specific information for some of the largest agencies in the country follows. Remember that salaries do not include additional money that can be earned for working overtime, on hazardous duty, or on less desirable shifts (taking the night shift can earn bonus pay). Many departments also add to your base pay after you have completed police academy training or finished a probationary period (usually your first year on the job). It is also possible to earn more each year for education: Having a college degree (or even some college credit) or getting advanced certification relating to your law enforcement work can mean extra income next year, depending on where you work.

Baltimore Police Department

http://www.baltimorepolice.org/

Average starting salary: $41,058 to $46,527

Benefits include: health insurance; paid vacation, holidays, court time, and overtime; investment plans; homeowner plans; free equipment; retirement after 20 years

Boston Police Department

http://www.cityofboston.gov/police/

Average base salary: $46,000

Benefits include: paid vacation, holiday, and sick leave; full retirement plan; educational incentives.

Chicago Police Department

http://www.chicagopolice.org

Average starting salary: $43,104

Benefits include: health insurance; paid vacation, holiday, and sick leave; tuition reimbursement, including advanced degrees; retirement plan; home purchase assistance; annual uniform allowance.

Dallas Police Department

http://www.dallaspolice.net

Average starting salary: $41,690 to $42,890

Benefits include: health insurance; paid vacation, holiday, and sick leave; life insurance; free equipment.

Los Angeles Police Department

http://www.lapdonline.org/

Average starting salary: $56,522 to $61,095

Benefits include: health insurance; paid vacation, holiday, and sick leave; pension plan; deferred compensation; compressed work schedule.

Miami-Dade Police Department

http://www.miamidade.gov/mdpd/

Average starting salary: $40,932 to $48,827

Benefits include: health insurance; life insurance; paid vacation; tuition reimbursement; pension plan.

New York City Police Department

http://www.nyc.gov/nypd

Average starting salary: $40,361 to $43,062

Benefits include: health insurance; paid vacation and sick days; educational incentives; annuity fund; Deferred Compensation Plan, 401K, and IRA; optional retirement for one-half pay after 20 years of service.

Philadelphia Police Department

http://www.ppdonline.org/

Average starting salary: $39,251 to $41,974

Benefits include: health insurance; paid sick leave, accumulated holiday and vacation time; pension plan, including deferred compensation.

San Francisco Police Department

http://www.sfgov.org/police

Average starting salary: $75,868 to $101,556

Benefits include: health insurance; paid vacation and sick leave; retirement eligibility at age 50, with a maximum of 90% benefit based on years of service.

Washington, D.C. Police Department

http://www.mpdc.org

Average starting salary: $48,715

Benefits include: health insurance; life insurance; paid holidays and additional duty; tuition reimbursement; homeowner plans; free equipment; retirement after 25 years of service; savings plans, including deferred compensation; free fitness centers.

The material benefits of a police career can be substantial. If you work for a municipal police department or state police department, your salaries will generally be among the highest in the city or state civil service system. It is not unusual to leave the academy after six or nine months earning close to $50,000 annually. An online study based on mean salaries at the beginning of 2007 found that the 10 states with the highest salaries for law enforcement personnel were New Jersey, California, Illinois, Washington, Nevada, Alaska, Connecticut, Pennsylvania, Colorado, and Oregon. Remember, though, that each police agency sets its own salary scale. Salaries are negotiated locally and different towns have different abilities to pay higher wages. Candidates are often surprised to learn that the salaries in the largest police departments are not the highest. Salaries are negotiated on a community's ability to pay, not on the number of police officers or the number of calls for service to which they respond. You might be very surprised to learn that a suburban community's officers make more than those in the large city nearby, and that a special jurisdiction police officer might make more than either of them. Remember also that salaries are sometimes closely related to local cost of living levels. A large paycheck may not go as far in a very expensive area as a smaller paycheck in a state where housing costs are lower.

Agencies covered by collective bargaining agreements generally provide officers with an annual pay raise during the life of a contract, usually three years. Sometime prior to the end of the contract period, negotiations with management will begin for a new contract; rarely will it be signed if no pay raise is included.

Despite a controversial history of unions in policing, today more than 40% of all police departments have a union or similar group that negotiates their labor agreements with either the police department or a unit of government set up specifically for this purpose, often called a law department, department of collective bargaining, or personnel department. The larger the department, the more likely it is to be unionized. In 2006, according to the Bureau of Justice Statistics, more than 80% of agencies that served a population over 1,000,000 had collective bargaining agreements, while only 13% of those serving populations under 2,500 had such agreements. Sheriffs' offices are less likely to be unionized, but here, too, size is a factor. State police agencies also operate under collective bargaining agreements. Since

2007, only two states, Virginia and North Carolina, forbid first responders, including police and firefighters, from joining unions.

Police officers also have substantial opportunities to earn overtime pay, generally at $1\frac{1}{2}$ times their hourly wage. Sometimes, if the overtime falls on a holiday or other special conditions are met, overtime might be paid at twice your hourly pay rate. The availability of overtime is one reason you will often see police recruitment ads that feature comments such as "earn up to" a certain salary a year rather than a specific dollar amount. This figure often represents the average of the available overtime that entry-level officers can expect to earn. It may also represent the addition of contractually agreed-to longevity increases that are added to your salary as you pass certain milestones such as completing the academy; or your probationary period (generally between one and two years); or reaching an anniversary date at three, four, or five years of service.

In addition to the substantial monies you will be able to earn directly from your agency, many departments have agreements that permit you to work another job (called moonlighting) during your off-duty hours. Although in many states police officers are not permitted to work where liquor is sold, in other areas nightclubs, concert venues, and sporting arenas and stadiums may hire off-duty police officers directly or may request they work through prearrangements with either the department or the union. While you are under no obligation to moonlight if you are not interested in additional income, the way many departments have organized this extra work makes it exceptionally easy to obtain for those who are looking for additional income.

JUST THE FACTS

Batter up! Baseball is a sport in which moonlighting policemen are on the payrolls. These officers are paid as part-time employees of Major League Baseball to help with security.

Many other benefits are provided by most police departments that do not call for you to do extra work at all. Most police departments, whether local, state, or federal, and most sheriffs' offices, provide health insurance to the officer and dependent family members, including dental and eyeglass coverage. In most agencies, this coverage extends even after you have retired, so it is in reality a lifetime benefit for you and your spouse, although children who reach a certain age will no longer be covered under your policies.

Virtually all departments provide paid vacation time; in some you are able to accrue as many as 30 days within your first or second year of employment. In many agencies you are permitted to carry over these days for years; some officers retire with so many days accrued that they remain on the payroll for six months or more after they have stopped working. Although many officers save their vacation time by choice, one of the few negative aspects of this benefit is that vacation time is usually approved in seniority order, which means that if you are a new officer, or if you have recently been transferred to a new assignment, you are unlikely to get your first choice of vacation dates. You can turn this into a benefit by travelling at off-peak periods, when prices are lower and crowds thinner.

In addition to vacation time, departments also provide sick and personal leave and generally 12 paid holidays. Once again, though, the needs of the department may prevent you from being off on holidays, although you will generally be paid at a rate of $1\frac{1}{2}$ or twice your normal hourly rate if you work on a holiday. Despite these generous amounts of time off, some families have trouble getting used to their officer being away from home on many holidays or having to work on many family occasions. To prevent family discord, some departments have added policies that allow officers to swap work days. This means that you can take off for any reason as long as another officer agrees to work your assignment so that the department is not short-staffed and is not faced with paying someone overtime to fill your vacant spot. It will be up to you to work a shift for your colleague to complete the swap.

Other benefits are less universal. A common one is a uniform allowance provided annually or an arrangement by which your agency provides you with virtually your entire uniform except for socks, shoes, and undergarments. Some agencies issue replacements for worn uniform parts; in other agencies you must purchase them yourself, but tax laws permit you to deduct from your income many items that you must purchase or maintain for work. Generally, most equipment is also provided, although some agencies expect you to purchase from an authorized vendor your firearm, handcuffs, and other police-specific equipment from your annual allowance.

Some departments offer tuition reimbursement for any college course in which you earn a grade of B or better; depending on the part of the country in which you work, some departments offer incentive pay for foreign language skills. Incentive pay may also be offered for education in excess of the minimum entry requirements, for being an emergency medical technician (EMT) or a paramedic, or for having skills that a particular agency has decided it needs.

Appendix B provides samples of job announcements from a variety of police agencies. Although each agency will have its own set of requirements, these are typical of the type of benefits you will be offered and the type of requirements you will be expected to meet to become employed.

RISKS

If police departments are offering such generous salaries and benefits, you might be wondering why positions are available at all. One reason that people often prefer not to discuss is that there are risks entailed in being a police officer. Yet, many of the risks are less about physical danger than about the stresses that come with the anticipation that danger could occur even when it does not.

Every police officer on television except those in comedy shows seems to fire a weapon at least once an hour. In reality, most police officers retire at the end of a 20- or 25-year career without ever having fired a weapon other than at the practice range. Certainly the vast majority have never had to fire at another person. An example of how fiction does not reflect fact can be seen in the activities of the New York City Police Department (NYPD), the nation's largest law enforcement agency, with more than 35,000 officers in all ranks. Shooting incidents in the department have been decreasing; according to the NYPD, in 2007 there were 111 police-involved shootings, 16 fewer (a decrease of 12.6%) than the previous year. Even these figures are misleading; of the 111 shootings, 45 were directed at criminals and 39 at animals, mostly dogs that police said were attacking them. Other reasons were 15 accidental firearms discharges and 12 that were defined as unlawful (including suicide, attempted suicide, and illegal shooting, firearms discharge by a person other than the police officer). The total number of shots fired was fewer than 600; quite different from the shoot-'em-ups that make up most fictional police dramas and the shows that claim to represent reality.

Does this mean police work isn't dangerous or that there are no risks? Not hardly. Policing can be a dangerous job and therefore not for everyone. Some of the danger is physical; there is an ever-present possibility of attack or of being asked to perform physically taxing tasks. Another kind of danger, though, is psychological and can come, as mentioned, from thoughts of the possibility of danger or, more likely, from the stresses of being exposed to negative events in the lives of others.

When asked about stress, officers most frequently mention the police or-ganization itself as a stressor. The need to make decisions on the streets or highways, but then to have those decisions so frequently questioned by the public, the media, and senior officers within the department, leads many of-ficers to feel they are constantly under scrutiny for even the most routine activities.

Facing physical danger in a job does not mean you must see yourself as Superman or Wonder Woman. It means, though, that you must put fears aside to when you run into a situation in which others are running away, and consider the safety of others before your own.

Each year, the National Law Enforcement Officers Memorial Fund (NLEOMF) adds to its wall in Washington, DC, the names of officers throughout the country who were killed in the line of duty the previous year. For the past 10 years, the numbers have fluctuated from 169 in 1998 to 181 to 2007. On the list are those killed feloniously, including those shot or attacked physically, and those whose deaths were accidental, perhaps in auto accidents while on duty either pursuing a suspect or killed while a suspect was fleeing other officers. Some officers drowned while trying to rescue people, some were attacked while serving civil restraining papers ordering people to leave their own homes.

The dangerousness of policing is sometimes questioned because a num-ber of occupations are comprised of workers who die at higher rates than police officers. These occupations include fishing, logging, and piloting air-planes. Yet these fields are dangerous in different ways; in these jobs worker deaths are likely to be the result of industrial accidents, whereas police are more likely to be killed intentionally or in situations that have gotten out of control but that, with the exception of the large number of traffic accidents, cannot by any stretch of the imagination be defined as accidents. While workers in other professions are expected to take precautions, such as undergoing special training or wearing safety equipment, none don a bullet-resistant vest each day to counter the possibility that they might be shot at or stabbed by an assailant.

Traffic Accidents

The one area where police officers are faced with accidental deaths similar to these other fields is traffic accidents, which annually claim the lives of more officers than do intentional or felonious actions by others. In 2006, for instance, more than half (73) of the 151 police officer deaths resulted from traffic accidents, while another dozen officers died in various other types of accidents. The number of officers killed in traffic accidents has increased over the past 30 years at the same time that the number of officers killed feloniously has been declining. The only exception to this pattern was 2001, when figures included those who died in the terrorist attacks on September 11.

Despite attempts by academic researchers and traffic engineers to determine the reasons for the increase, no one factor has been determined to be the major culprit. Some attribute the problem to faster cars and the greater mobility of both police and criminals, some indicate that police officers—particularly young ones—may drive carelessly, particularly when pursuing suspects.

Another unproven theory is that many large city police agencies, in an attempt to recruit more local residents, have done away with the requirement that candidates have a driver's license before entering the police academy. Although defensive driving has long been taught at police academies, the need to teach basic driving skills to new police officers has resulted in many rookies who are assigned to patrol in marked police cars but are inexperienced behind the wheel. If you live in a large city, there is a good chance that you have read a newspaper article about police officers becoming involved in one-car accidents either during pursuits or in trying to control their vehicle and the emergency equipment simultaneously. You might even have found the articles amusing, but if you are successful in your job search you will learn how difficult it can be to control all the emergency equipment in a patrol car and control the steering wheel at the same time.

Another reason for the accidents might be that police officers are likely, despite regulations to the contrary, to drive without wearing their seat belts, either because they anticipate having to exit their vehicles quickly or frequently or just because the amount of equipment they carry on their belts makes seatbelts more uncomfortable for them than for the average driver. Departments have attempted to counter the increase in vehicle accidents by limiting the situations in which officers are permitted to pursue suspects and by increasing disciplinary penalties for driving without a seatbelt.

Stress

Another risk—less deadly perhaps, but one that may ultimately affect a person's quality of life or even longevity—is stress. Stress can come from any number of sources and certainly is not unique to policing. A number of factors, each of which individually may not occur only in policing but are combined in policing, may form an unusual set of circumstances that are associated with stress. Street-level police work, whether in uniform or in plainclothes, opens an officer to threats of danger at any time. Will the next call, one that initially appears routine, result in violence when someone turns out to have a gun or a knife or to refuse, even if unarmed, to be taken into custody peacefully? Will a routine call to assist a sick person turn violent when the person's relatives refuse to permit emergency medical personnel into the home?

Even though an undercover operation was carefully planned and all possible attempts were made to control the setting and personnel on the scene, might the informant have lied, might the address have been incorrectly recorded, or could one or more of the subjects become suspicious that the undercover may be a cop? None of these questions can be answered in advance.

A third area of stress may have nothing to do with potential danger to the officer individually but is a type of system overload from being exposed to the troubles of others. Witnessing and having to respond to the troubles of others can be stressful even to bystanders. As someone thinking of a career in policing, have you considered what it might mean to see battered and brutalized children or spouses in domestic disputes? Will you think too long about your own children or spouse being placed in a similar situation? Officers may also be in situations where they will be exposed to dead bodies; many times those bodies may be dismembered, burned, bloated, or otherwise maimed. Your internal fortitude will be tested.

In the last 30 years police departments have become more attuned to stress. Officers are encouraged to display emotions after a situation has been concluded, and counseling after being involved in a shooting or having spent days or even weeks at a disaster scene, is today an accepted part of policing. Part of this changed view is a deeper understanding of post-traumatic stress disorder (PTSD), which may result in an officer's own life unraveling after exposure to too many emergencies or after hiding his or her emotions for too long. Bowing to an image of strength, and concerned that their problems will not be kept confidential, many officers refuse to rely on department counseling services, but departments continue to offer them with assurances they will not negatively affect career outcomes.

Police departments have not only addressed danger by trying to determine if there are patterns behind violent encounters or whether traffic-related deaths and injuries can be minimized or how to counteract the most obvious forms for stress, they have also tried to minimize some of the routine stress associated with shift work and other working conditions that are part of policing. They have also developed peer counseling and professional programs to address occupational stress.

SHIFT WORK

Shift work, which can be defined either as being expected to report for work at different times during a workweek or working nights, overnights (sometimes called the graveyard shift), or even weekends is not unique to policing but it is something that all police officers face at different times in their careers. Some effects of shift work that have been detected are fatigue due to too little sleep or irregular sleep; irritability; and eating and digestive problems. Changing shifts frequently or irregularly increases these problems because often, just as the body becomes adjusted to a particular work/rest schedule, it is changed.

In addition, shift work can affect not only the officer, but also the officer's family. Family members are required to tiptoe around the house when an officer is sleeping during the day, eat irregularly in order to have meals with a parent, or be forced to spend time with caregivers other than their parents. Although shift work is common in many fields, police officers are required to change their shifts more often than others or to be on call frequently for real or anticipated emergencies.

In past decades, it was not uncommon for officers to work so-called rotating shifts, which might have required changing shifts as often as every three or four days. Those types of schedules are less common today as departments have moved to steady shifts. This may mean an officer works the same tour for months or even for as long as he or she cares to once a certain level of seniority has been achieved. Where shifts are still changed regularly, officers will be likely to work the same duty hours for two weeks or a few months, which allows for body rhythm changes to be less abrupt and provides an opportunity for families to establish more stable routines.

The same theory is used in determining non-work days. Since policing requires that someone always work weekends, departments have developed schedules where officers remain on the same hours but move their days off based on a system that permits everyone to have all or part of the weekend off a set number of times in, for instance, a six-month period. Many departments, with encouragement from their unions, permit officers to swap days off, so that a colleague can work in your place if you have an event you really want to attend.

Stress-related concerns have also played a role in changing from an eight-hour to a ten-hour day. Officers work longer hours, but fewer days, allowing them more personal and family time. Almost without exception, departments that have changed to four days of 10-hour tours to accommodate the most common 40-hour workweek have found that officers favor this system. As the costs of commuting increase, the 4-day workweek is a financial as well as a psychological benefit.

THE POLICE ORGANIZATION

Despite concerns about stress brought on by exposure to violence, when police officers are surveyed they most often list as their major stressor the police organization itself. The bureaucratic nature of policing is inherently contradictory; police officers must make decisions on their own (commonly referred to as exercising discretion) while on patrol, but are also subject to what can appear to be small and insignificant rules which they had no role in developing. Some of these include wearing your hat when outside of your patrol vehicle, or wearing short-sleeved shirts only between June 15 and September 15. Failure to observe such rules can result in disciplinary action.

Within the last decade, as tattoos have become commonplace, many departments have ruled that none can be visible to the public. This could mean having any body art you have obtained removed in a costly and painful way or, at a minimum, wearing long-sleeved shirts in climates that might reach over 100 degrees. Are you prepared to give up your individuality for the sake of uniformity? How difficult it may be for you to do this is a common stressor in police work.

Women and minority group members may face additional stress. Although the extreme behavior of many male police officers that occurred in the 1960s, 1970s, and early 1980s, when women were far fewer in number, has abated, women may be subjected to various forms of sexual harassment. Currently, gay, lesbian, and transgendered police officers are the more likely subjects of taunts or isolation, particularly in departments that remain more rigidly military in their discipline and demeanor. Yet many departments have recognized fraternal associations of these officers and they now participate in activities with the older associations. Appendix A provides a listing of the many professional and fraternal associations in policing.

Minority officers may also feel the effects of tokenism. When you are one of few among a much larger group, there is a tendency to be placed under the microscope, to have your actions more openly commented on, and to face stereotypical expectations about how you will act in certain circumstances. Tokenism can be hurtful in two contradictory ways. If you behave in a way that sustains the majority group's stereotype, you are rejected as inadequate. If you behave in a way that violates the stereotype, the majority group sees you as an exception to the rule, not as an individual, and the members of your own minority may resent you for being viewed differently. Either way, this is an exceptionally stressful situation. Agencies are trying to address this through diversity training and also through recruiting more different categories of minorities so that the workplace is not so fractured by these ideas.

Does this mean that all of these stressors will affect each officer? Not at all; but it is better to be aware of the realities of what you may be faced with.

CHAPTER three

TODAY'S COPS: WHO THEY ARE AND WHAT THEY DO

Police work is about multitasking. Juggling 10 things at the same time is not unheard of. You may be gathering the descriptions of the perpetrators and direction of flight, putting the information over the radio, requesting an ambulance for the victim, requesting the supervisor, cordoning off street corners or subway stations, preparing required forms, all in a matter of minutes. Your method is the difference between a criminal captured and getting away.

—Police sergeant assigned to training

SOME POLICE agencies advertise their jobs as the career of a lifetime or a job like no other. Others advertise the opportunity to make a difference in your own life or the lives of others.

If you are reading this book, you have already decided that policing is something you want to pursue. But how much do you really know about the routine activities of police officers? Are you, like so many others, influenced by television and movies, where every moment brings great excitement in the fight against crime? Has your decision been influenced by the those same shows, with their numerous car chases and foot pursuits through alley-ways, over fences, and even, in some urban dramas, jumping from roof to roof like a mountain goat or a gazelle?

In truth, you are more likely to be called to a home where there is a dis-oriented adult or a sick child than to one in which someone is armed and dangerous. In urban areas, particularly in a publicly funded housing devel-opment, you might be more likely to be called when the elevator is out of service or the toilet overflows than because someone is selling drugs or as-saulting another resident. Similarly, in a leafy suburb comprised of single-family homes, on a quiet midnight tour you might be given a list of families who are away and told to shine your flashlight into their garages, backyards, or front windows to make sure no unauthorized persons have taken up resi-dence or committed a burglary.

Regardless of the size and income level of your community, you are likely to be called to a park if teenagers are noisy or appear to be drinking. You might be able to convince them, using tact rather than force, that it is time to go home. If your community has a curfew, you might be better able to assure compliance. If they have been drinking, depending on their ages and your department's policy, you may have to call their parents or guardians to pick them up. In some very service-minded agencies, you may be expected to bring them home, even if you resent becoming a babysitter and chauffeur.

If your community has a strip mall or large shopping mall, private secu-rity officers may call you for assistance for the same type of call you just handled in the park.

In each of these occurrences, you will be responding because someone has called in a complaint. This is what police call "answering calls." These calls normally come into your agency or to a regional dispatch center. The dispatcher, in turn, contacts you via your car radio or handheld portable radio and, after providing you with whatever information he or she re-ceived, sends you to investigate and resolve the problem.

Depending on the size of your agency, the dispatcher might have selected you because of special skills you exhibited that the dispatcher was aware of. More likely, and certainly in a large agency, the dispatcher will have no idea about you other than that you were available; you were what is called "in service" to receive the next call. If you are already involved in a handling a problem, you will be considered "out of service," or not available to take an assignment until you complete your current one. If you work in a busy department, you will have calls coming one after the other. The dispatcher or your tour supervisor, generally a sergeant, will encourage you to complete your calls quickly so that you are available for future calls. In a quieter jurisdiction, you may be encouraged to take a bit more time and try to resolve an issue so that you or others are not forced to respond to the same problem on a regular basis.

Whatever the nature of the call for service, on your way to the location you will have to review what you know about this call—but just as important, what you do not know. If it is a call about a sick person, who might be there who might not want to comply with the need to call an ambulance or have the sick or injured person removed from the home? If the call is about juveniles, how many are there, and might one or two decide to show off for the others by trying to defy your authority? Should what seemed like a routine incident turn threatening, you will have to change your tone of voice, your body language, and your tactics quickly.

Other calls to which you might be dispatched have a higher potential for danger from the start. A call to a burglary in progress means you might come face-to-face with a criminal. You will get your adrenaline pumped up, only possibly to learn when you arrive that there is no burglar. The "burglar" might be someone out walking a dog who the caller had never seen before or might have been a tree branch that frightened the caller enough to look like a person. A less innocent finding might be someone who seems to be studying the area to commit a future crime, something you must handle with tact and without violating the person's rights if you are unsure of what his or her presence means. Possibly "the burglar" is someone committing an offense that is less serious under your jurisdiction's penal law, such as exposing his or her private parts. Each of these possible scenarios requires a different response from you and is an example of why discretion is such an important part of police work.

In addition to the emotional ups and downs each call generates, each will also generate required paperwork. Whether you find a burglar or a tree branch, you will be expected to file a report documenting how you received the call (by dispatch), what time you received it, what time you responded, what you did when you got there (including the correct address, correct spelling of the names of anyone you spoke with), and what time you completed the call and went back into service to be available for the next call. Many departments have tried to simplify the reporting requirements by putting computer terminals in the police cars so that you can input the information immediately or when you are not on a call. Others, generally the largest departments in the least wealthy communities, are unable to do this. You will be expected at the end of your tour of duty to use a shared computer or typewriter to complete all the reports on all your calls before you leave. This a major reason why police officers indicate paperwork as one of their major stressors.

There will be times when you will not be answering calls. During this time you will do what is call patrolling, which means riding or walking around a designated area (your beat) looking for crimes or other problems. If you find any of either, you will notify the dispatcher of your activities. This is so the dispatcher knows whether you are available for calls he or she received and also so that someone knows where you are and what you are doing in the event you need assistance from other police officers. Work you generate on your own is most often called pickup calls, because you have picked them up yourself rather than waiting for them to be sent. Situations you generate on your own are also called "pickup jobs," "obs" (for observed activity), or "self-initiated activities."

If you patrol in a marked police car, many of your pickup calls will be traffic-related. If you work for a state police agency, particularly a highway patrol department, you would expect this to make up a larger portion of your workload, but the same is true for other types of departments. You may be assigned to monitor an intersection where a large number of complaints have been received about people ignoring stop signs or traffic signals. Or you might be assigned to a section of a roadway where a large number of accidents have occurred. If you stop someone, you will need to have a plan in case the person turns violent. If the person remains calm, you will be able to exercise a certain amount of discretion as to whether to issue a verbal or written warning or to write a citation. Some of this may depend on your department's policies, but often the decision will be yours. You will hear many stories, some completely beyond belief, as to why the driver was speeding or, ignored the signal. Some will be so outlandish that you will look forward to getting back to the stationhouse to share the story with your colleagues.

Not all traffic stops are humorous, though. Like domestic dispute calls, they are often unpredictable and can turn violent at a moment's notice. In either situation, your demeanor and your actions may be influenced by whether you are patrolling alone or are in a patrol car with another officer.

These descriptions of typical encounters with members of the public are not meant to discourage you or make you believe that you will never be functioning as the heroic crimefighter, but rather to reinforce to you that a minority of calls to the police concern serious crimes. Even in high crime areas, it is very likely that you will be mostly involved with traffic enforcement, handling a variety of minor crimes, and providing services to the community such as helping injured or sick people; providing information, instructions, or directions; or advising residents of other government agencies that can better handle their problems, preferably during normal business hours.

This description has focused on local police agencies. As indicated, in a state police or highway patrol agency, your tasks will be more traffic-related. Even in state policing, though, if you are assigned to patrol a small community without its own local police department, you will be more involved in calls similar to those described than to mostly stopping motorists on the highway. If you are in a highway patrol agency, your involvement with traffic enforcement will be the largest of the agencies described. Special jurisdiction police agencies may have many similarities with local departments, but also major differences. Some special jurisdictions operate exactly like village, town, or city departments. Within their jurisdictions, a Native American reservation, a college campus, a bus or train station, a park or nature preserve, for example, they are the local police and they respond to identical situations.

JUST THE FACTS

Over the past few years alone, the Internet has exploded into one of the most commonly used tools for networking and communication, but it has also become a new frontier for law enforcement all over the world. Doing research for a report on chemistry could lead to instructions on how to make explosives. The convenience of buying everything from the comfort of your own home could turn into a financial nightmare when sensitive information is left where hackers and identity thieves can find it. The cyber world is rife with all kinds of illegal activity, from piracy to child pornography and exploitation to drug trafficking, and governments are desperately trying to crack down on perpetrators of these and other crimes.

Since the ascendancy of widespread computer use, law enforcement agencies from the ground up have developed cybercrime task forces to tackle these newfound issues. New laws have also been enacted to aid the catching and sentencing of cyber criminals. However, due to the possible national and international ramifications of computer-related misconduct, this field is still slowly being explored and tested.

For all patrol officers, distinct from detectives or other specialists, arrest is a small portion of their workload. Even in very large, high-crime cities, many police officers make few or no arrests. Some of this has to do with the nature of the calls they receive, but some of it reflects their eagerness to look for situations during their nonassigned times. You may believe that you will always be hunting for an arrest situation, and early in your career that may be true, but it may not remain true for 20 or 25 years.

Just as there are differences among officers, different agencies also have different operating styles. Some departments will encourage you to make arrests or become more involved in curtailing criminal activity; other departments will stress greater community involvement through non-arrest strategies. While departments may change their focus depending on the leadership, you will have to fit your own style to the style of your agency.

THE HIRING PROCESS

If you are truly serious about becoming a police officer, the hiring process starts years before you apply for the job. Much of your suitability will depend on your background investigation. If you have a record of arrests, have been in numerous motor vehicle accidents, have a record of domestic violence, have been fired frequently for cause, have a less than honorable discharge from the armed services, have used drugs regularly or frequently, or if you have a bad credit record, it is likely that you have disqualified yourself for employment even before you begin. Any one of these things may not be an automatic rejection from every agency, but if you nodded yes to more than a few of them, you should consider whether a career in law enforcement is possible for you.

If nothing—or very little on the list—pertains to you, you are ready to consider the formal applicant hiring process. Many departments claim, although no one has actually verified the claims, that they go through more than 100 applicants for each new officer they hire. Remember that these odds do not include those who read the minimum qualifications and never began the hiring process. But it is also important that despite the number of applicants who do not make it into a police department, many departments today are eager for applicants and many around the nation are actually having trouble filling existing vacancies.

This means that if you are serious about a law enforcement career, are able to meet eligibility requirements, and pass the steps in the selection process, you have an excellent chance of becoming a member of a law enforcement agency. Your chances will be greatly enhanced if you are flexible. If you can consider a wide range of agencies and are able to move around your region or even to another section of the United States you will have a greater number of opportunities for employment. If you are committed to staying close to home and your local police department is not currently hiring, you should seriously consider any special jurisdiction agencies in your area. You may be pleased to learn that these agencies are hiring and may offer salaries and benefits comparable to those offered by your local police department.

Your opportunities for employment are also enhanced by learning as much as you can, which is one reason you are reading this book. And your chances are even greater if you start early, follow instructions carefully, ask for an explanation of anything you do not understand, and answer all questions truthfully.

Because of the different types of law enforcement agencies and the large number of agencies within each category, it is difficult in law enforcement to use the words "always" or "never." Although there are some variations in the hiring process, there are enough common elements to provide you with a preview of what to expect when you apply for a law enforcement position. Since the largest number of job openings are in local policing, this discussion adheres most closely to those requirements but points out the major differences for other types of law enforcement agencies.

MINIMUM ELIGIBILITY REQUIREMENTS

The hiring process has two interrelated parts. The first part involves what are generally called minimum (or basic) eligibility requirements. These include U.S. citizenship, a minimum and maximum age you must be at the time you are appointed (not the same as the time you take the exam); vision requirements; whether or not a driver's license is required prior to hiring, and educational requirements. For local agencies, the minimum education is most likely to be a high school or General Education Diploma (GED) and for most federal agencies it is most likely to be a four-year college degree (either a bachelor of arts or a bachelor of sciences). Increasingly, state and local agencies are also requiring some college education.

Minimum eligibility requirements mean just that; they are the least qualifications you will be expected to have met either before you apply for a position or before you are accepted for employment. Applying for a position and being accepted for employment are not the same thing.

Departments differ on whether you must have met the minimum requirements at the time you take the entry exam or at the time you are actually appointed and assigned to attend a police academy. Some job announcements make the difference very clear. Others are written in government jargon that you may need to reread more than once before you are confident you are able to follow the instructions. Many applications include a telephone number or e-mail address to contact if you are unsure how to proceed. Do not be embarrassed to take advantage of this. It is far better to ask questions first than to discover later that your application has been rejected for something that could easily have been done correctly.

Since many departments charge a fee for taking the entry exam, it is important to find out whether you must meet the minimum standards when you take the test or when you are notified you have passed the test and asked to submit your credentials for a background investigation. Do not make assumptions; some departments will permit you to have not yet met some qualifications but to have met others at the time you take the test. For instance, you may be allowed to take the test even if you are too young to be appointed. Similarly, you may be permitted to take the test if you have not yet met minimum college education requirements. If you pass the exam and have not yet met that minimum when you are called for an interview or to begin the background investigation, though, your application will be put aside until you have achieved the minimum number of credits. Even having your application put aside can be complicated. In some large agencies, you may lose hundreds of places on the civil service list and have to wait years to be called again. Other, often smaller, agencies simply put your application aside until you notify them that you have met the minimum requirements.

A major reason for the different rules has to do with the length of time the hiring process involves. Very large agencies may test thousands of candidates at once and it may take up to two years before candidates learn whether they have passed the written exam, completed the background investigation process, and been offered a job. Additionally, some departments believe that allowing candidates to take the test during their teen years will encourage them to maintain a lifestyle that will not prevent their being hired once they get older. The idea is that the possibility of a police career will help young people maintain a good driving or credit record and a drug-free lifestyle, and generally remain law-abiding so that they do not lose what they have already invested in a law enforcement career.

JUST THE FACTS

As a student, you can join the American Criminal Justice Association, as well as some other professional organizations. The ACJA offers scholarships and other awards and holds an annual student essay competition. They also hold job fairs at their national conferences. Reach them at acjalae.org. Look for other organizations online using the keywords "law enforcement organization."

United States Citizenship

One nearly universal requirement is U.S. citizenship. A few urban departments and some smaller agencies in the southwestern states have considered changing this but since being sworn in as a police officer requires taking a constitutional oath, it can be anticipated that departments seeking to eliminate the citizenship requirement will face legal challenges from applicants who are citizens but are not selected.

If you are a non-citizen military veteran, you will probably be allowed to take the test based on the expectation that your citizenship application can be expedited if you are accepted for employment. You may also be permitted to take the test if you have already applied for citizenship and have completed some of the initial processing.

If you do not fall into either of these categories and you are not a citizen, you should inquire whether you will be permitted to take the entry test and to participate in any pre-employment activities.

Age

Age is another area where departments interpret the minimum eligibility standards differently. Some will permit you to take the test as young as age $16\frac{1}{2}$ with the understanding that if you pass the exam, your application will not be processed any further until you meet the minimum age requirements to become a police officer, which is as young as 18 in some states and generally 21 in most others. Federal agencies differ on this policy, so be sure to check the agency you are applying to carefully before proceeding with your application.

The decision to permit applicants to take the test years before they are eligible for appointment is in part a reaction to the shortage of police applicants. As with the decision to permit early testing to encourage a healthy and lawful lifestyle, departments believe that permitting applicants to test early would interest people in police careers before they had been lured to other professions. This is a particular concern of departments that require two or four years of college since potential applicants will generally be older and will have been exposed during their education to careers they might not have originally considered.

Many departments began cadet programs in the 1970s, often to attract minority youths to policing. These programs, too, were based on the theory that positive interactions with police officers, as well as taking the entry exam early, would increase the numbers of successful minority applicants. Most of the programs were discontinued before their successes could be measured, but they did result in changing many age eligibility requirements for taking the police test. Many of these cadet programs have been modified to attract college students with a combination of work-study or paid work until they are eligible for employment.

Education

Educational requirements may also have to be verified prior to your being permitted to take the written exam. A few departments require that you meet the minimum requirement before the written test; most, though, knowing that it may be a considerable time from applicant testing to test results, will permit you take the test with the understanding that, as with citizenship and age, if you pass the exam, your application will be frozen until you meet the education requirements.

Residency

Some agencies require you to be a resident of the area. Some indicate preferences for those who live in the agency's jurisdiction. There is a difference between a residency requirement and a residency preference.

A residency requirement means that you must live either in the jurisdiction of the agency or in a surrounding area that will be specified as part of the position announcement. The Mount Vernon Police Department announcement in Appendix B is an example of an agency that has residency requirements for appointment. Its requirements are typical of agencies that do not mandate that you live in the town in which you will be working, but do require that you live in specified surrounding areas.

Read the job announcement carefully. In some instances you must be a legal resident of the area at the time you take the test; in other instances you will be expected to move into the designated area prior to accepting the position. Although not universal, a sheriff department will often give preference to county residents unless there are an insufficient number of applicants from within the county. Federal agencies have no residency requirements, although if you are hoping to stay in your home area, you will most likely be disappointed. Generally, upon completion of training new special agents are not returned to the area from which they were recruited.

There are a variety of ways in which a residency preference may operate. Some agencies provide extra points on the entry exam to applicants who have passed the test and live in the designated area. Almost always, you must score a passing grade without the preference. Rarely will the preference be used to bring your score high enough to be considered for employment. The three or five points that may be added to your test score may not seem like much. However, for a test in a large urban area that may attract thousands of applicants those few points may make a very large difference in your position on the civil service list; they might even result in your being scheduled for processing a year or more earlier than you would have been without the preference. Some agencies provide what is in effect a signing bonus for those who meet the residency preference, providing them with a small stipend in addition to the basic salary. Some departments hire from a large regional civil service list, but, rather than taking candidates in order of their scores, are permitted to go through the list to first select residents of their communities.

JUST THE FACTS

Check the rules carefully for the agencies to which you are applying. You do not want to invest time and possibly application fees only to learn that you will not be allowed to take the exam. Most police agencies are as eager for you to follow the instructions as you should be. They do not want to waste your time and money or their own by having to cull from the applicant process those who are ineligible. The Denver, CO, Police Department, for instance, posts on its website a 26-page booklet that can be read online or printed out; it provides a detailed discussion of all entry requirements and the types of skills or abilities that can bring you extra points on the application or extra salary if you are hired.

Specifically, be sure whether the rules on the job announcement must be met at the time you apply for the test, at the time your selection processing begins, or at the time you are appointed to the position. In large agencies, the time differences may be measured in years, making this an important factor in your decision.

THE SELECTION PROCESS

The real selection process begins after you have met the minimum eligibility requirements. If you already know the actual or type of agency to which you will be applying, your process will be somewhat easier than for than for those who are just beginning their job research. As you saw, policing is made up of many categories of agencies and many, many agencies within each category. Some selection process steps are fairly standard across all agencies; others are not. Some agencies' websites are very specific about eligibility requirements; others less so.

Although there are great similarities among agencies, no listing of hiring requirements and eligibility standards will be the same for all agencies or even for a particular category of agencies (i.e., local, state, federal, special jurisdiction).

This explanation of the selection process is not all-inclusive, but it is sufficiently broad to give you a deeper understanding of the hiring process. The most common steps include submitting a completed application form, taking and passing a written test (generally multiple-choice), passing a physical agility/ability test, passing a background investigation, and a psychological and medical evaluation. Additional steps that some agencies rely on include an oral interview and a polygraph (lie detector) test.

In a review of selection procedures published by the Department of Justice's Bureau of Justice Statistics (BJS) in 2003, the most common screening procedures used by municipal police departments were (in their order of use): a background investigation, a personal interview (often conducted by the investigator assigned to do your background investigation, but sometimes a more formal process before a panel comprised of two or three members of the department), a medical exam, a drug test, a psychological evaluation (which may include a written test and an interview with a psychologist), a physical agility test, a written aptitude test, a polygraph exam, and, lastly, used by very few departments, a voice stress analyzer.

The list can seem intimidating, particularly if you are the first among your family or friends to consider a law enforcement career. Remember, though, that the steps take place over a period of time, giving you time to do research and, as you pass each phase, to gain confidence that you will achieve your aim. If you are attending a college with a police studies or criminal justice program, learn if the career counseling office has people to assist you in the process. Also, if criminal justice-related majors are a major focus of your college, you have probably taken some of these courses and know that some of your professors have worked in law enforcement. Most will be happy to assist you with pointers and to reassure you as you move through the selection process.

Application and Written Exam

The first step you will be asked to complete is an application. If you are applying to a large department, this step must be completed before you will be scheduled to take a written exam. In addition to providing you with entry to this exam, your initial application may ask detailed questions that will be checked against later questionnaires you will complete for a background investigation. Under no circumstances should you lie. False responses are grounds to exclude you from the applicant pool regardless of how well you score on the written exam.

Generally, the larger the agency, the more likely it is to rely on a written aptitude test as the first step in the hiring process after an application has been completed. Some agencies schedule written tests only every few years due to the costs involved. Some also may still have an existing civil service list of applicants but are planning ahead for future hiring. A few agencies have what are called "walk-in tests," which means they give tests regularly (weekly, monthly, etc.) to applicants who have previously applied or even to some who literally walk in on the exam date.

If you are attending a college with a police studies or criminal justice program, check with the career counseling office; many departments schedule their written exams on local campuses. Because of the availability of police jobs in many parts of the country, many agencies offer tests at campuses where they can expect to attract a large response. If you are able to consider relocating for a position, check the requirements for these agencies and do some research to determine whether you might want to live in the area. The Internet has made it feasible for you to learn about colleges, the real estate market, schools, and the availability of jobs for family members who may be relocating with you.

Regardless of whether the website of your chosen agency indicates a test is anticipated, if you are permitted to do so, you should file an application to assure that you will be notified in the event a test is scheduled. Within recent years, a number of departments have started to accept online applications; this is an efficient way to apply and also lets you apply to as many departments as may interest you with only a few clicks of your mouse.

Here, too, though, there is considerable variation. Some agencies allow you to download the application form, print it, and submit the completed application by mail. A few agencies allow or require you to fill out the application directly online. While this may be a faster method, if you are not a good typist or if you do not have all the relevant material available, you may discover that you are unable to comply with the instructions. If the application must be completed online, try to review it before beginning the process so that you are confident that you can answer all the questions.

Some sheriffs' offices and many police agencies that are comprised of 25 or fewer officers may not require you to take a written exam to be considered for a position. Check with the agency directly or on its website for instructions. Particularly in rural counties, an interview with the sheriff or undersheriff may result in an offer of employment pending completion of the background investigation and the police academy.

If you decide to make in-person inquiries at an agency that does not require a written exam, remember to dress appropriately in business casual attire. Less formal than business attire, which traditionally is a suit for men and a dress or pantsuit for women, business casual attire is worn at many advanced police training courses. This is the only time you should appear in business casual attire, which is generally is defined as dress slacks and a collared polo or sports shirt for men and a skirt and blouse, daytime dress, or pressed slacks and a collared shirt for women. At all other times that you visit your department when formally requested to do so, a man should wear a business suit and a woman a business-appropriate dress or a pantsuit.

Do not plan ever to visit the agency when you are wearing jeans, cut-offs, flip-flops, or similar casual clothing. You might see officers getting out of their personal cars dressed like this to report for work, but they are already employed and you are not. It is not uncommon in smaller agencies that the chief or sheriff or a high-ranking officer may be in the public area of head-quarters when you make your inquiry. First impressions, particularly in an agency that bases it hiring decisions heavily on an interview, can mean the difference between acceptance and rejection. You don't want to risk closing the door on employment before you even begin.

If you have applied to an agency that administers a written test, make sure to appear on the correct date and earlier than the time printed on the exam card. Depending on the size of the agency, you may be one of thousands of applicants and there may be long lines at the testing locations. Come early, bring whatever tools you have been advised to have with you, and follow all instructions carefully and fully.

A civil service test administered by a police agency follows strict rules. When the test time begins, the door will be shut and those not already in their seats will be denied entry. Unlike high school or college, there will not be a teacher who has known you for a long time and may be willing to let you in late or give you a few extra minutes at the end to complete the exam. One of the first shocks for police applicants is that few exceptions are made; while no one wants to steal your uniqueness, you must also get used to being one of many who are all expected to follow the same rules.

Prudence suggests that once you have received your information about the test site, you make a trial run from your home to the location to judge how long it will take you to get from there to the site. However long it takes, add at least an additional hour or two to account for delays along the way and for long lines at the test site. If you treat the test time the same as you would any plans to travel by airplane, you are likely to be on time and relaxed when the test paper is placed on your desk.

Depending again on the size of the agency for which you have tested, it might take quite a while for you to get your test results. The reasons may vary, but whatever they are, you can expect to eventually receive a notifica-tion with your test score. If you are informed that you did not pass, you may receive information on how to appeal your result. In the interest of brevity, this discussion assumes that you passed the test and have been placed on what is generally called the eligibility list.

Physical Agility

For many years, the step immediately after receiving notification you had passed the written exam was the physical agility test. In the past, some agencies were stricter about the physical agility test than they are today, although generally state police agencies continue to use your ability to pass a rigorous set of physical tests as a major consideration in the selection process.

When agencies also maintained strict height requirements, the physical agility test site was where you were measured to assure you met the minimum standard and that your weight was proportional to your height. Along with being measured and weighed, you were put through physical testing including primarily running, sit-ups, push-ups, and chin-ups.

Much of this has changed. Primarily in response to lawsuits in the 1970s and early 1980s brought by women applicants and shorter, slighter men, height and weight requirements have been replaced with a somewhat less vigorous agility exam. For instance, many agencies have eliminated chin-ups, replacing them with agility tests that are more comparable to the daily activities of a police officer. Examples of what you may be asked to do include rapid acceleration drills, which might include a short climb over a wall, hurdle, or hedge or running through or over a storm drain, gulley, or fence, or running or darting through a crowd. You might be asked to drag a dummy of a certain weight a certain distance to test whether you would be able to rescue an inert person in an emergency. You might also be asked to climb a ladder or squeeze the trigger of the firearm used in the agency to measure your wrist, hand, and finger strength and control. The physical agility test for state police agencies will very likely be more strenuous than these examples and you will be less likely to get a second chance to pass if you are unable to complete all aspects of the agility exam.

If you do not receive detailed instructions on what comprises the physical agility test when you are notified that you passed the written exam or when you are called in for this phase of the process, your first step should be to check your agency's website. Many agencies provide detailed descriptions of their physical agility tests and also tips on preparing for the test.

If you are overweight, you should begin a weight control program immediately upon learning you have passed the written exam. Possibly you should consider starting a weight reduction and health care program even before taking a written test so that upon passing you can begin more strenuous training for the physical agility test. It would be wise to begin a physical conditioning program and to inquire whether your agency provides guidelines on what will be expected of you in the academy and how you can begin to improve your physical abilities.

A number of agencies, especially in California, where many local police agencies continue to maintain physical agility requirements that are more stringent than elsewhere in the country, allow you to participate in a structured program run by department physical fitness instructors. This helps you not only to get into good physical condition, but also to learn the techniques that can help you successfully complete the run, wall-climb, or other agency-specific tests. These programs were originally implemented to help women prepare for the physical agility tests because they were failing them in far higher percentages than men. The programs were so successful that men sought entry; today, where such program exist they are open to all candidates willing to invest the time in pretraining.

The pass rates for physical agility tests have been falling in many police agencies. The reasons suggested are a more sedentary society, with more young people playing computer games than participating in sports, and the general rise in obesity throughout the country. To assist candidates in meeting their requirements, some departments have gone to lengths previously unheard of, including providing applicants who fail the test with fitness club memberships and an opportunity to retest, allowing applicants who come close to passing to enter the academy and be retested prior to graduating, and even allowing candidates who fail the physical tests at the conclusion of academy training to be recycled into the next training academy rather than be terminated from employment.

Even if you are in excellent condition and the test instructions do not seem difficult to you, do not take the agility testing lightly. Remember that you will likely have to perform the various feats under timed conditions in front of physical fitness instructors and that you are very likely to be nervous, knowing that your future employment will depend on your score. It is also important that you listen carefully to all commands. Some exercises must be completed in a particular sequence for you to get credit for them and some may test not only your overall physical condition, but your ability to follow instructions under stressful conditions.

Visual Acuity

Vision requirements have changed drastically within the last 20 years. At one time, candidates who wore glasses were unlikely to be hired even if their vision was correctable to 20/20. Departments would not consider applicants who wore contact lenses, but eventually improvements in soft lenses convinced departments that these lenses would not pop out in an altercation or result in blurred vision under extreme weather conditions. Today most agencies accept applicants whose vision is correctable to 20/20 or 20/40 by either contact lenses or eyeglasses.

Applicants must also have normal peripheral vision (meaning you have a normal range of vision to the left and to the right) and may not have any eye disease. One vision requirement that has not changed is that you cannot be color-blind. The logic of this is apparent; responding to traffic signals and emergency flashers could easily be impaired and the ability to describe anything based on its color would be impossible.

Background Investigation

The background investigation is a crucial part of the selection process. Although it may seem less intimidating than the physical agility testing, it may actually be more crucial because there is little or no leeway for a second chance. While some departments may permit you to retake portions of the physical agility exam and even encourage you to work out to do better, once you have completed the forms your investigator will use to complete your background investigation you will have few opportunities to correct other than the smallest discrepancies.

Also, while you can improve physical or mental conditioning for the future, it is impossible to undo the past. Your life will be placed under a microscope and errors in judgment made many years ago may permanently alter your chances for police employment.

Among the aspects of your life that will be checked are your school records, all your places of residence going back 10 years or more, medical and military records, past employers, use of drugs or excessive use of alcohol, your driving and credit histories, arrests or other recorded contacts with the police, and any information that may lead the investigator to question your suitability to be a police officer. The investigation will be based primarily on information you provide through forms you will be asked to fill out, your fingerprints, and photos. You will be asked to fill out and sign release forms (waivers) so that the information can be released to the agency. While you may be given an opportunity to correct minor errors, anything that can be interpreted as a deliberate falsehood will result in disqualification. Keep in mind that standards regarding background issues evolve over time and something that isn't quite stellar today, might not be as important tomorrow. Moreover, as time passes, earlier transgressions are often overlooked, especially if the candidate has done something with his or her life. However, lying is always a disqualification, so it is better to tell the truth and risk disqualification for that than to lie.

When you meet your investigator for the first time, dress as you would for any job interview; a suit and tie for a man, a business-style dress or suit for a woman. This is the same way you should dress if your agency conducts an interview as part of the applicant process. Avoid excessive jewelry and anything that jangles and creates a distraction from what you have to say. You want to make sure that your first impression shows that you are serious about this job and that you understand the importance of the background investigation. Turn off your electronic devices when you meet with your investigator or anyone else at the agency, and certainly during your interview. These are not the times for your cell phone to blare out your favorite tune when your best friend calls to find out how things are going.

Just as you did for the written exam site, you should make a test run to where you will meet your investigator. Arriving late, no matter how professional you might look or sound once you arrive, detracts from your image. Although your investigator may not be much older than you are, never address anyone by first name and remember to use courtesy titles such as Sir or Ma'am. Speak clearly, avoid slang and obscenities, and make eye contact with your investigator and any other people who address you directly. Ask your investigator for a business card or to spell out his or her name. This is a person you will be interacting with on more than one occasion; if you are required to telephone or send additional information, you want to be sure you know who to ask for and where to address forms or other items you may be asked to submit.

Psychological and Medical Evaluations

These evaluations are generally done after completion of your background investigation. Both are costly to your agency but are meant to save money and problems by assuring that you will be mentally and physically able to perform typical police tasks.

The psychological exam is generally administered in two parts. The first part is a paper-and-pencil test during which you will answer a few hundred questions that ask, among other things, about your personal attitudes and how you describe yourself. Many of the questions ask the same thing in different wording; this is to assure the honesty of your responses. Whatever you may be told by others, it is almost impossible to cheat on a psychological test. The way the questions are worded make it highly unlikely you will be able to fool the exam.

Although the questions may seem odd, many of the tests used by departments have been devised specifically for police or other emergency service candidates. The test is scored to determine your suitability on the basis of whether you are hiding having abused drugs or alcohol, your self-management skills (do you get unnecessarily angry over small issues), how well you can be expected to take direction or work in groups, and your intellectual ability to understand different sets of circumstances.

You will also at some point be scheduled to meet with a psychologist or psychiatrist who will interview you to determine whether you meet the requirements for a law enforcement position. You will generally receive one of three recommendations: recommended, recommended with reservations, or not recommended. It is up to your agency to determine how closely it chooses to follow these recommendations. Most agencies are unlikely to hire a candidate who receives a negative evaluation, not only to protect the candidate from emotional problems but also to protect the agency from lawsuits should you become involved in a controversial situation and the results of a negative evaluation are made public.

The medical exam is intended to evaluate both your short-term and long-term health. The medical exam is not the same as physical agility testing. Your agency wants to know if you are healthy enough to perform police-related tasks. Are you able to stand for long periods of time without passing out? Are you able to sit for long periods of time without getting severe cramps in your extremities? If you become fatigued easily you might be unable to withstand the rigors of some assignments. Keep in mind, however, that the medical exam portion is sometimes challenged by applicants—the agency's doctor may say no, but a private physician may disagree.

The long-term concerns revolve around whether you are prone to injuries or ailments that would shorten your career. Early retirements are costly to a police department; not only do most officers who retire early receive a more substantial pension than they would in the private sector, the department must now begin the costly and time-consuming selection process to replace you. It is neither in your nor the department's best interests for you to begin a career that is likely to end prematurely.

A new requirement that many departments include under physical conditions and/or lifestyle is that you be a nonsmoker or nonuser of tobacco products. Originally applied to on-duty conduct, within the past decade many departments have made this a condition of both on- and off-duty conduct. Even when smoking was permitted, officers could not smoke in public; this was an image issue rather than a heath concern, though. This meant that officers who smoked generally did so in their patrol cars or around the stationhouse, resulting in nonsmokers complaining about the dangers of secondhand smoke. This often resulted in a ban on all on-duty smoking. Eventually, primarily in response to medical reports on the dangers to overall health and the rising costs of insurance due to smoking-related ailments, departments began to prohibit smoking at all. Court cases have upheld the prohibition. Today in some agencies using legal tobacco products is as much as cause for dismissal as is the use of illegal substances.

Personal Interview

The personal interview can take many forms. In some agencies, your time with your investigator and with the professionals conducting your psychological and medical exams will also be counted as interviews because those individuals will be asked to assess your communication skills and your responses to predetermined questions.

For some agencies, the interview is a more formal event during which you will meet with a board of individuals who will ask you specific questions about yourself and why you want to be a police officer or who may probe more fully into issues raised by your background investigation. Board participants may also ask you to describe a stressful situation and how you handled it or they might give a typical policing scenario and ask you what you would do (this is generally called *a hypothetical*). The board may be comprised only of police personnel or may include a number of civilians from other agencies or from community-based groups. Generally, the interview will be taped for later review or in the event board members disagree on your handling of the interview.

What are they looking for? A number of things, including how you present yourself, how you address the group, whether you answer the questions specifically or avoid them, and whether your answers are appropriate for the hypothetical situation you were asked to resolve. Remember the recommendations for meeting with your investigator—dress appropriately and address board members by title or as Sir or Ma'am. Make eye contact with the questioner and with other board members when they speak to you. Try to avoid such verbal pitfalls as beginning each sentence with "um," "you know," or "well." Remember to sit fully in your seat without fidgeting, playing with your jewelry or your hair, or scuffing your feet on the floor. These and similar distractions show a lack of self-confidence or self-control and are likely to weigh in the board's assessment of your suitability for a position.

These pointers may seem obvious, but many people are often unaware of the physical or verbal tics they have. Even if you cannot rehearse the actual interview, you can begin to make yourself aware of how you seem to others and you can begin to eliminate these annoyances well in advance of the personal interview.

Other Selection Mechanisms

Depending on the agency considering you for employment, you may be asked to submit to a polygraph exam designed to determine whether you have been truthful throughout the applicant process. A few agencies also use voice stress testing, which is another way of determining the honesty of your responses. Although many think of the polygraph as a new invention, it was first used by Chief August Vollmer in Berkeley, CA, in 1921.

Polygraphs (or lie detector tests) are administered by trained operators. What you say is less important than the measurement of certainly bodily functions during your replies. Basically, the polygraph device records changes in physiological functions such as breathing, heart rate, and blood pressure. Not all states permit results of a polygraph to be used in court, but they may be used in pre-employment screening. If you refuse to take either the polygraph or voice stress test it is unlikely that you will be hired.

One of the most recent concerns of police departments has been officers who are heavily tattooed, particularly if the tattoos appear gang-related or can be interpreted as having racial or sexual overtones. Even if the tattoos are not in themselves controversial, a number of agencies have indicated that none can be visible to the public. This could mean that if you have one or more tattoos on your arms, you could be asked to wear a long-sleeved shirt even during the warmest months of the year. Because departments value uniformity, though, you might be asked to remove or cover your tattoos so that you are not wearing a different uniform from your peers. When a product becomes available commercially it usually means a trend has been detected. Law enforcement magazines have begun to carry ads for sleeves that look like skin to cover highly visible tattoos. Although special agents are not uniformed, federal law enforcement agencies have also recently been discouraging any visible tattoos.

You may find it ironic that as tattoos have become more mainstream and more people, including women, have been getting inked, police departments have become more sensitive to this issue. Part of the reason is that as tattoos have become more common, they have also become more noticeable, resulting in some public complaints about the image of heavily tattooed officers. Many police agencies also believe it detracts from the image of professionalism they are trying to convey.

Although there has been less discussion about visible piercings, it was as recently as the 1970s that police departments began to permit post-style earrings, first among women officers and then men when some complained that the policy of permitting women to wear any earrings while men could not was discriminatory. Dangling earrings worn by either women or men are prohibited because they are a safety hazard. The early policies on earrings that were not safety hazards tended to reflect a generation gap. Most of the senior-level male police setting policy found it difficult to accept that a man would consider wearing an earring. Policies are less well-defined on other piercings, but you should anticipate that any policies that are developed in this area will closely mirror policies on tattoos.

What to do if you have a tattoo? The mature approach is certainly not to get any additional ones. Since having a tattoo removed is costly and painful, it would be wise to wait until you are under serious consideration for a position or have been made a conditional offer of employment to learn the details of your agency's policy and to find out what steps you will be asked to take to comply with that policy. What if you have numerous piercings? Since no one will be concerned about the small holes that may be in your nose or eyebrow, the wisest course of action would be to leave the jewelry at home.

JUST THE FACTS

It can cost a police department $60,000 or more to recruit, hire, train, and equip an officer. For many departments, this amount is double the officer's first year salary, which is why agencies use such a thorough application process. They need to eliminate those who won't be able to handle the job well before they attend the academy.

EDUCATION VERSUS TRAINING

Many people confuse education and training; but they are very different. Education is knowledge-based; it is defined as a body of academic knowledge that is most often learned in a classroom setting. Knowledge is theoretical rather than how-to. Using a police-related example, you can study the laws pertaining to arrest without ever taking someone into custody or without having any knowledge of how handcuffs work. You can study the laws and court cases pertaining to the use of deadly force without ever having to aim a firearm and shoot it at someone.

Training, on the other hand, is skills-based. It is how-to and covers what you need to know to perform a specific task or group of tasks. Learning *when* to take someone into custody involves knowing the law and recognizing that you have witnessed a law being violated; learning *how* to take someone into custody involves knowing how to approach and talk to a person who is resisting or is agitated or intoxicated and knowing how to place handcuffs on a person in way that is safe to you and to the person being taken into custody.

If the agency to which you are applying has education requirements, you will be expected to have achieved these on your own. The training you need to be a police officer will be provided to you by your employer.

Education Requirements

With the exception of federal agencies, according to data collected by the Bureau of Justice Statistics, more than half (63% in 2000) required only a high school diploma or General Education Diploma (GED) for employment. About 37% required some college, most often 60 credits or a two-year degree; fewer than 5% required a four-year degree. Agencies requiring education beyond a high school diploma, while still a relatively small percentage, have increased substantially since the 1990s. Additionally, minimum requirements do not always accurately reflect actual hiring practices. Although formal studies are sparse, many agencies have indicated that more than half their applicants have educations beyond the minimum requirements for employment. (See Chapter 4 for more information on education.)

Training

Your first assignment as a newly hired officer will be to attend and successfully complete a police academy. The words *police academy* have become synonymous with basic training as a police officer. At certain times during your career you will very likely return to the police academy for supervisory, management, or specialized training. But when people in policing refer to the academy they are referring not only to a physical place, but to the initial training officers receive. When an officer says of another officer, "I went to the academy with her," this means they received their basic training together.

TYPES OF POLICE ACADEMIES

Just like everything else you have now learned about careers in law enforcement, police academies also come in a variety of formats.

Most academies are run by police for police. Student officers (generally called rookies) have already been hired by a police agency and are on the payroll of that agency. These academies will be either commuter or residential. Large cities most often open their academies only to their own rookie officers, who commute daily from home. State and federal agencies have residential academies at which you must live for the entire training period. Groups of smaller local and special jurisdiction agencies generally train their officers in regional academies that are similar to large city academies except that the officers come from many different agencies. Unless the area is so rural that officers must travel too far to commute, regional academies are generally commuter institutions.

A newer, far less common type of academy has developed to permit candidates who are not hired by a police department to attend academy training and then seek positions based on their certified police status. This type of training, often called "alternate route," has aroused considerable debate and is not accepted by all agencies, but more than 30 states offer it as an option for candidates who have not yet been hired by a police agency.

Commuter Academies

Large city police departments have their own academies; generally, only officers from that department attend, although sometimes smaller or special jurisdiction agencies may be invited to send officers to this academy. If not, these agencies' officers are eligible to attend regional academies generally administered by a state's police training council (sometimes also called the office of police officers standards and training) and held at locations throughout the state, generally on a quarterly basis or, in more rural areas, as the need develops.

Commuter academies, whether run for or by a single agency or for multiple agencies, maintain hours and schedules similar to high schools. You will be expected to attend on a regular schedule, usually five days a week except for specialized instruction, and you will go home each night. You will be expected to arrive and depart in a uniform usually designed for rookie officers so that you are not mistaken for a fully-sworn, armed officer. Your transportation to and from the facility will be up to you. The distinct uniform, most often a different color from the agency's regular uniform, is particularly important if you rely on public transit to reach the academy. Your agency will warn you repeatedly not to get involved in police work during your training period. While in rare events rookies who violate this rule and do something particularly heroic may be honored, it is more likely that you will be disciplined and possibly even fired for violating this rule.

Your workday in a commuter academy will be structured like school. There will be classroom training, gym and physical training, and, as you progress through the program, swimming, emergency rescue techniques, defensive driving, and firearms instruction. Almost all your instructors in a single-agency academy will be members of your department; a few outsiders may deliver specialized lectures.

Generally, if your recruit class is larger than 30 officers you will be broken into smaller groups (usually called squads). Squads generally elect a leader or someone is appointed to the position by the academy staff. Often someone a bit older or with prior military or police training, this rookie is responsible for the squad's behavior. The position is often sought after and conveys a certain prestige of being chief among equals.

Your squad will become your reference point for your training experience. Generally, you will line up together for uniform inspection and to receive the day's instructions. You will attend classes and physical training with your squad, take your meals together, study together, and participate together in any extracurricular activities. Many police officers remain close their entire lives with those who were in their recruit class squad.

If your department is not a large urban or state police department, it is likely that you will be assigned to attend a regional police academy. Here there will be student officers from many departments, including local area police departments, sheriffs' offices, and special jurisdiction agencies. The instructors, too, will likely come from a variety of agencies; usually from the departments that send their officers to that academy.

Regional academies, like single department academies, are recognized by the state's police training council and must meet all the same requirements as single agency academies. These are generally run along the lines of commuter academies, but since they serve a number of departments, the actual training may focus more on state-mandated requirements and state laws and less on the day-to-day procedures of a single department.

Nationally, and within a single state, regional academies will have the most variation among them. Although the curriculum is mandated by the state, the tone of these academies may differ somewhat from the single-agency or residential academies. Sometimes this is due to where classes are held. In other cases this is because the participating departments have different views on the importance of a military-style training environment.

Rookie officers attending a regional academy generally also wear distinctive attire, most often uniforms. Your rookie uniform may be the same for all classmates or may reflect individual department preferences. Since some regional academies conduct classes on community college campuses, they may make some attempts to minimize the differences between rookies and other students. Even where student officers are uniformed, the discipline of a formal morning uniform inspection or of marching or running from one class to the next may be minimized. Since rookie officers will most often eat in the campus dining area, although they generally stick together, they will not be expected to move to and from their tables as a unit and may be encouraged to mix somewhat with the other students to break down community barriers toward the police.

Consider the reality; if you were to attend a regional academy that was conducted on the campus where you had recently been a student, it might be difficult for you to maintain strict segregation from your former classmates. It might benefit your police agency for others to see you as remaining an integral part of the community. Also, what better possible recruitment tool might there be for your agency than for your friends to see you on campus, working to achieve your career goals but continuing to be a member of the larger community?

Residential Academies

If you are a newly hired state trooper or highway patrol officer, your academy experience will be less like high school and more like a boarding school or military training. You will very likely be expected to live at the training facility. Some departments will allow you to go home each weekend, others may limit your visits home similar to basic military training.

The residential academies resemble military training in other ways, also. Although many no longer expect recruits to live in a barrackslike structure, you can expect to share your living space with other recruits and to share toilet and shower facilities with members of your class. Private rooms with your own personal electronic devices, laptops, and television sets are not part of the accommodations. You can also expect to take all your meals with your class or squad. Dining is generally cafeteria-style, and, particularly in state police academies, squads must eat together, at the same time at the same table. Unlike your high school or college cafeteria, table-hopping or sitting with those you have chosen is not an option. Mealtimes are short— no more than 30 minutes. You will be expected to take your tray to a discard area, often with your squad rising as a group, and to immediately reassemble at a designated point to return to class, again as a unit.

Evening activities are preplanned for you and undertaken as a group. Depending on the academy, there may be gym or running activities for all, or academic study groups. In some academies, you will be assigned evening activities based on your individual progress. If you are lacking in physical agility, you will probably spend additional time in the gym. If you are falling behind in academics, you may be assigned a study partner with whom to review areas in which you are deficient. While this helps you to remain at the same level as your classmates and may prevent you from failing the program, that some applicants are unprepared for the level of oversight of their activities and their time.

Residential academies can help to bond officers to one another and to create an especially close esprit de corps but they present a number of potentially stressful situations for older applicants, particularly those with families and children. Many features of residential academies were developed when state policing did in fact closely resemble military training and when applicants were between the ages of 18 and 29. Today, in response to federal laws pertaining to age discrimination, or agencies having added college requirements, many rookie officers are older than those of past decades. Although some residential academies have loosened some of their more military aspects, they are considerable different from college dormitories and they have changed less than many of their applicants have.

Because today's applicants are often older and college-educated, some observers of policing have found fault with the residential academies. Others believe this style of training is one reason state police agencies attract fewer women applicants and that both women and minority applicants find being away from home a stronger disincentive than do majority-group applicants. This view is based on the belief that women, particularly those already in their mid-20s, are more likely to have family and childcare responsibilities and are, therefore, less able to attend a police academy that takes them away from home for long periods of time. For minority applicants, a possible negative aspect is that residential academies are often located in a rural portion of the state, far from areas from which these applicants tend to be recruited. Not only are these rookies further from home, but the surrounding community is often one that is very different from their residential areas.

In addition to not seeing your family, if you have accepted a position with a department that sends you to a residential academy you will be unable to maintain any outside activities such as work or school. While commuter academies also discourage and in many cases prohibit you from continuing to work or attending school, some make an exception if you are taking online courses or if you work only part-time in a family-owned business. These exceptions are not made in residential academies, which, again, are the norm for state police agencies and for federal law enforcement positions.

Depending on where you live, your state's police academy may not be too far from your home community, and you may be permitted to leave on weekends, particularly in the second half of your training period. Being away from home may be particularly burdensome at the federal level. Training for federal law enforcement takes place at only three or four locations around the nation. With the exception of a facility in Virginia, the others are in rural areas, often on former military bases. Even if you were permitted to return to your home each weekend, the logistics and costs could make this an unachievable aim.

These caveats are not meant to discourage you. State police and federal law enforcement agency appointments are sought-after positions by police applicants. Knowledge is power, though, and knowing what to expect in any undertaking will help you to make decisions that will prevent you from taking wrong turns as you decide on the details of a career in policing.

Alternate Route Academies

The vast majority of the more than 600 police academies that operate nationwide follow the patterns of either the commuter or residential academies. Within the past decade, though, a new form of academy has developed. It has become known as "alternate route" training because it presents a completely different way of entering the police profession.

The alternate route academies, which exist in more than 30 states, allow those interested in a police career to complete the required mandatory subjects and physical training to become a police officer on their own time and at their own expense. Typical requirements are similar to those for joining a police department. Generally, students must be the same ages as are required by the individual state for police certification, must be U.S. citizens, must be in good physical and mental heath, and must have completed a minimum level of education, either a high school diploma or 60 college credits.

Many of the programs require a student to attend full-time during weekdays. Some may operate evenings and weekends to attract candidates who must continue to work until they complete the training and obtain a law enforcement position. Completion of the course does not guarantee police employment, but most schools that offer the program in conjunction with the state's police training commission provide a list of agencies that will hire officers who have completed the training. Generally these will be local police departments and special jurisdiction agencies. Few state police or highway patrol agencies accept alternate route graduates and federal agencies will assign all candidates, regardless of prior police training or experience, to one of its training locations for basic special agent training.

Although some scholarships are available, the costs of this training are borne by the student. Once selected, a student may be expected to pay a non-refundable fee (in 2008, the fee, for example, at the Essex County, NJ, College Police Academy was $1,000) for a background investigation, a psychological and medical exam, and for drug testing. Once these have been completed, there are tuition fees may run into thousands of dollars (Essex County, NJ, charges $3,000 tuition for a 21-week program, payable upon acceptance, plus about $1,200 for uniforms and equipment).

Why are these programs controversial? The first reason is that they are completely different from the historical method of delivering police training to candidates who have already been hired. Concerns voiced by police agencies are that the candidates are not sufficiently vetted because a community college or regional training facility will not or cannot do as intense a background investigation as an employing agency will do. Some have voiced concern that some attendees will be anti-police attending a program to learn how to create problems and lawsuits for departments.

Another concern is that this will create elitist police departments, with only those able to pay their own way being able to obtain employment. There are fears that if the alternate route gains in popularity, departments will curtail their own training to save the time and money required for doing a full-scale applicant selection process paying an officer to attend the police academy. The advocates of alternate route counter this by arguing that true professions except candidates to become trained on their own and to be ready to begin work when they are hired.

If you are able to consider funding yourself through the alternate route training program, make sure that you learn which agencies in your area accept the training and which fees, if any, are refundable if for any reason you decide to discontinue the program.

THE ACADEMY EXPERIENCE

Regardless of the type of police academy you attend, you are joining policing at a time when training has been enhanced. Although training itself is not new, it was only in the 1950s that states began to set minimum training requirements for police officers. Since that time, the number of hours and the range of subjects that are taught to rookies have increased substantially. Many training programs were initially as little as 300 hours, which, divided into a 40-hour week, meant programs that were as short as $7\frac{1}{2}$ weeks, or barely two months. Today, the average number of hours of basic training for police officers is about 650, although in some programs more than 1,400 hours (35 weeks, or more than eight months), including the academy and the field training experience, are included in the total.

The number of hours you attend the basic academy and the subjects you are taught are generally defined by a police training authority with statewide jurisdiction. This is to assure that all police officers receive the identical mandated training. Academies may offer more than the state-mandated training, but they may not offer less. Generally, large departments, often defined as those in cities with populations over 100,000, tend to provide longer academy training programs than smaller departments.

A detailed list of topics taught in basic police academies is available on the websites of many of the state training councils. Their similarities are striking. For example, taking two mainland states that at opposite ends of the continent, New York State mandates 635 hours of training and California mandates 664 hours. Although the listing looks very different, the difference in hours is spread across so many subjects that the actual number of hours per topic is quite similar. Sex crimes are taught for two hours in New York and four hours in California; physical fitness and wellness consumes 65 hours in New York and lifetime fitness 44 in California.

The length of time, though, does not always reflect the breadth of training, since, as indicated, much of the curriculum is state-mandated. Large departments, with their own academies, are able to add hours to train rookie officers on the departments' unique policies and forms. Smaller departments that rely on regional academies generally do this during the field training period. Because larger departments often police a more diverse population, they may devote extra hours to teaching new officers about the histories and cultural differences among the citizens they will police. Some invite representatives of these communities or groups that focus on cultural diversity to provide lectures and role-playing exercises for students. In the past decade, as urban departments have also eliminated the requirement that officers enter the academy with a driver's license, they have also had to add hours for driver education and practice driving before being able to begin defensive driving instruction.

By now you have come to understand the pitfalls of generalizing about many aspects of policing, but academy curricula at the state and local level share a number of commonalities across jurisdictions. The Bureau of Justice Statistics reported that in 2002 the largest single area of instruction in police academies was firearms skills (a median average of 60 hours), followed by investigation techniques and self-defense (45 and 44 hours, respectively). The only other single topic to which more than 40-hours were devoted was criminal law. Other areas of study include domestic violence, constitutional law, cultural diversity, ethics and integrity, and community policing.

Using the medians above gives a candidate an idea of what will be studied, but not necessarily how it will be learned. Of the four largest areas outlined in the BJS study (firearms, investigations, self-defense, and criminal law), only the last one is primarily classroom-based book learning. For the other three categories, officers will be exposed to legal aspects (i.e., when it is permissible to use force, when it is permissible to use deadly force, when it is permissible to undertake a vehicle chase); they will also participate in such hands-on training as loading and cleaning a firearm, shooting at a variety of types of targets, handling evidence and taking measurements pertaining to, for instance, an automobile accident. The use of hands-on technique is generally what differentiates education from training; education can be defined as the why or why not, while training may be seen as the how to or how not to.

Hands-on training is also the method for most defensive tactics training and for physical fitness and physical agility training. During your time in the academy you should expect to run almost daily, starting at distances of up to a mile and increasing to five or more miles while also lowering your times. Because this area of training and ability plays a larger role at the state police level, many individual department websites provide a detailed description of the level of fitness you will be expected to have in order to enter the academy, milestones at various key training points, and what is considered the minimum level of achievement for graduating from the academy. In addition to running milestones, there may be goals for swimming generally and for water rescue maneuvers; for first aid (including Red Cross certification or the opportunity to obtain an emergency medical technical [EMT] certification); for delivering babies or extricating victims from accidents, fires, or explosions.

Some theory is taught in the area of defensive tactics, but here, too, much of the training will involve hands-on practice, often with or against class-mates. You can expect to use one another to learn on, whether it is boxing, handcuffing techniques, or various come-along holds. Generally instructors will try to pair students of like size and weight, but if you are smaller than the average police officer, you will be encouraged—if not forced—to prac-tice on someone larger than you to provide you with the experience you will need on the streets.

The more sedentary aspects of training will be more like high school or college. You will read books or manuals, listen to lectures, and see films or computer-based presentations on the material. This type of training is com-monly used for learning the law, department policies and procedures, how to explain your cases to prosecuting attorneys, and how to testify in court. Lectures will be supplemented by role-play, during which you might be asked to make believe you are a suspect trying to lie to or mislead a police officer, or, in reverse, the officer trying to get at the truth. On another day you might act the role of a non-English speaker trying to explain an inci-dent in which you are the victim of a crime; or you might be an attorney questioning your classmate harshly to determine whether the facts you stated surrounding the arrest you made are accurate.

Less interactive lecture supplements will include filling out blank copies of the forms required when a theft has been reported to you, or a motor ve-hicle accident, or when you have made an arrest. Rookies are often amazed at the number of forms they must learn to fill out; it is a major aspect of the job and one that is rarely portrayed on television and in movies. Paperwork requirements remain one of the major complaints officers have throughout their careers.

Eventually, after months, if you successfully complete all the training re-quirements, you will graduate from the academy. Your family will be invited to a ceremony much like a high school or college graduation. There will be speeches, generally by the police chief, sheriff, or academy director, possibly by local politicians or other dignitaries. Some of your classmates—possibly even you—will receive awards. The rookie officer with the best academic average will be recognized and probably receive a book or a plaque. The of-ficer with the best physical agility tests or who has shown the most improve-ment since the beginning of training will receive an award. The student with the best firearms scores will be recognized and possibly receive a firearm donated by a local vendor, and the best overall student will also be recognized. Again similar to a school graduation, a rookie valedictorian may speak, often recalling how naïve you all were when you entered the academy only a few months ago and how much more confident you now feel in your own abilities despite what may be concerns (or even fears) about what the future will bring.

In your mind you are ready to go out and fight crime. But in the minds of the leaders of your agencies, you are ready only for the next step in your training—assignment to a field training officer who will watch and guide you and report on your progress before you are actually permitted to exercise your police authority and the discretion that comes with it on your own.

FIELD TRAINING

Field training developed later than academy training. Until the 1970s it was, if it existed at all, an informal system in which rookie officers were assigned to work with more experienced officers. Often for no more than a few days, the new officer mostly learned the geographic area and watched how the more experienced officer dealt with members of the public in a variety of situations. The experienced officer was often not selected on the basis of being an appropriate role model. Working the same days and hours as the new officer was many times the major selection criterion.

As with many changes in police training and accountability, a more organized style of field training developed in California, specifically the San Jose Police Department. Begun in 1972, this has remained the most widely recognized and imitated field training program. Although it seemed revolutionary at the time, the San Jose model basically formalized having a new officer observe a more experienced one by selecting field training officers on the basis of their abilities, rather than their availability, and having the training officer formally evaluate the recruit-trainee on a number of specific tasks.

From this sprang a number of variations and a training specialty of field training officer (FTO). Today many field training programs require the recruit-trainee to work with a number of different FTOs. To ensure that the officer is exposed to different styles of policing the trainee may be moved through different areas of the city. There may be considerable disruption to your personal life, since you will be expected to work days and nights, weekdays and weekends, all with the aim of exposing you to different experiences early in your career. In some programs, the evaluation of the trainer may play a role in whether you pass a prestated probationary period and are permitted to remain employed as an officer. Shifting a rookie officer to a number of trainers prevents personality conflicts or intangible dislikes from having too great an influence on a young officer's career. This is a real concern of agencies; the San Jose program was developed in part in response to a sex discrimination suit by female officers, who alleged that they were being judged on criteria other than their abilities as police officers.

Generally, the more formal a field training program, the longer it will last. Simply patrolling with a more experienced officer may go on for only a week or two. The current San Jose program continues for 14 weeks and includes periods of patrolling with periods of instruction and a predetermined rotation pattern. Most programs fall somewhere between these parameters.

The final step before becoming a full-fledged member of a law enforcement agency is completion of the probation period. Although not directly a training phase, a probationary period may last up to two-years, depending on state civil service law or on the department's negotiated union contract. The average probation period in police departments is one year and it may or may not include the time spent in academy training. Whatever the time frame, during this period an officer may be fired without a hearing without cause, a legalistic way of saying for any reason.

THE POLICE OFFICER SUITABILITY TEST

This chapter has taken you from civilian status to fully trained police officer—from the start of the applicant process to successful completion of your probation period. Along the way you have undoubtedly learned some things you had not anticipated would be expected of you. Although it may not have taken you very long to read the chapter, the actual process may take you three years or more.

To get a better idea of whether you and law enforcement are a good fit, consider taking the Police Officer Suitability Test that concludes this chapter. It is another tool to help you decide whether you want to invest years of your life in pursuing what may seem like a dream job, but may not be the best possible fit for your talents and personality.

Wanting to be a police officer is one thing; being suited for it is something else. The following self-quiz can help you decide whether you and this career will make a good match. There is no one "type" of person who becomes a police officer. Cops are as varied as any other group of people in their personalities, experience, and styles. At the same time, there are some attitudes and behaviors that seem to predict success and satisfaction in this profession. They have nothing to do with your intelligence and ability—they simply reflect how you interact with other people and how you choose to approach the world.

These "suitability factors" were pulled from research literature and discussions with police psychologists and screeners across the country. They fall into five groups; each has ten questions spaced throughout this test.

The LearningExpress Police Officer Suitability Test is not a formal psychological test. For one thing, it's not nearly long enough; the Minnesota Multiphasic Personality Inventory (MMPI) test used in most psychological assessments has 11 times more items than you'll find here. For another, it does not focus on your general mental health.

Instead, the test should be viewed as an informal guide—a private tool to help you decide whether being a police officer would suit you, and whether you would enjoy it. It also provides the opportunity for greater self-understanding, which is beneficial no matter what you do for a living.

Directions

You'll need about 20 minutes to answer the 50 questions that follow. It's a good idea to do them all at one sitting—scoring and interpretation can be done later. For each question, consider how often the attitude or behavior applies to you. You have a choice between Never, Rarely, Sometimes, Often, and Always; put the number for your answer in the space after each question. For example, if the answer is "sometimes," the score for that item is 10; "always" gets a 40. How they add up will be explained later. If you try to outsmart the test or figure out the "right" answers, you won't get an accurate picture at the end. So just be honest.

Please Note: Don't read the scoring sections before you answer the questions, or you'll defeat the whole purpose of the exercise!

How often do the following statements sound like you? Choose one answer for each statement.

Never	Rarely	Sometimes	Often	Always
0	5	10	20	40

1. I like to know what's expected of me. 20
2. I am willing to admit my mistakes to other people. 10
3. Once I've made a decision, I stop thinking about it. 5
4. I can shrug off my fears about getting physically hurt. 40
5. I like to know what to expect. 20
6. It takes a lot to get me really angry. 5
7. My first impressions of people tend to be accurate. 10
8. I am aware of my stress level. 40
9. I like to tell other people what to do. 40
10. I enjoy working with others. 40
11. I trust my instincts. 20
12. I enjoy being teased. 5
13. I will spend as much time as it takes to settle a disagreement. 20
14. I feel comfortable in new social situations. 20
15. When I disagree with people, I let them know about it. 40
16. I'm in a good mood. 20
17. I'm comfortable making quick decisions when necessary. 40
18. Rules must be obeyed, even if you don't agree with them. 40
19. I like to say exactly what I mean. 40
20. I enjoy being with people. 40
21. I stay away from doing exciting things that I know are dangerous. 5
22. I don't mind when a boss tells me what to do. 40
23. I enjoy solving puzzles. 40
24. The people I know consult me about their problems. 20
25. I am comfortable making my own decisions. 20
26. People know where I stand on things. 40
27. When I get stressed, I know how to make myself relax. 5
28. I have confidence in my own judgment. 40
29. I make my friends laugh. 40
30. When I make a promise, I keep it. 20

31. When I'm in a group, I tend to be the leader. _20_
32. I can deal with sudden changes in my routine. _20_
33. When I get into a fight, I can stop myself from losing control. _10_
34. I am open to new facts that might change my mind. _20_
35. I understand why I do the things I do. _20_
36. I'm good at calming people down. _40_
37. I can tell how people are feeling even when they don't say anything. _40_
38. I take criticism without getting upset. _10_
39. People follow my advice. _20_
40. I pay attention to people's body language. _40_
41. It's important for me to make a good impression. _40_
42. I remember to show up on time. _40_
43. When I meet new people, I try to understand them. _20_
44. I avoid doing things on impulse. _20_
45. Being respected is important to me. _40_
46. People see me as a calm person. _20_
47. It's more important for me to do a good job than to get praised for it. _40_
48. I make my decisions based on common sense. _20_
49. I prefer to keep my feelings to myself when I'm with strangers. _40_
50. I take responsibility for my own actions rather than blame others. _5_

Scoring

Attitudes and behaviors can't be measured in units, like distance or weight. Besides, psychological categories tend to overlap. As a result, the numbers and dividing lines between score ranges are approximate, and numbers may vary about 20 points either way. If your score doesn't fall in the optimal range, it doesn't mean a failure—only an area that needs focus.

It may help to share your test results with some people who are close to you. Very often, there are differences between how we see ourselves and how we come across to others.

Group 1—Risk

Add up scores for questions 4, 6, 12, 15, 21, 27, 33, 38, 44, and 46.
TOTAL = _200_

This group evaluates your tendency to be assertive and take risks. The ideal is in the middle, somewhere between timid and reckless: you should be willing to take risks, but not seek them out just for excitement. Being nervous, impulsive, and afraid of physical injury are all undesirable traits for a police officer. This group also reflects how well you take teasing and criticism, both of which you may encounter every day. And as you can imagine, it's also important for someone who carries a gun not to have a short fuse.

- A score between 360 and 400 is rather extreme, suggesting a kind of macho approach that could be dangerous in the field.
- If you score between 170 and 360, you are on the right track.
- If you score between 80 and 170, you may want to think about how comfortable you are with the idea of confrontation.
- A score between 0 and 80 indicates that the more dangerous and stressful aspects of the job might be difficult for you.

Group 2—Core

Add up scores for questions 2, 8, 16, 19, 26, 30, 35, 42, 47, and 50.
TOTAL = 275

This group reflects such basic traits as stability, reliability, and self-awareness. Can your fellow officers count on you to back them up and do your part? Are you secure enough to do your job without needing praise? Because, in the words of one police psychologist, "If you're hungry for praise, you will starve to death." The public will not always appreciate your efforts, and your supervisors and colleagues may be too busy or preoccupied to pat you on the back.

It is crucial to be able to admit your mistakes and take responsibility for your actions, to be confident without being arrogant or conceited, and to be straightforward and direct in your communication. In a job where lives are at stake, the facts must be clear. Mood is also very important. While we all have good and bad days, someone who is depressed much of the time is not encouraged to pursue police work; depression affects one's judgment, energy level, and the ability to respond and communicate.

- If you score between 180 and 360, you're in the ballpark. 360+ may be unrealistic.
- A score of 100 40 180 indicates you should look at the questions again and evaluate your style of social interaction.
- Scores between 0 and 100 suggest you may not be ready for this job—yet.

Group 3—Judgment

Add up scores for questions 3, 7, 11, 17, 23, 28, 37, 40, 43, and 48.
TOTAL = 215

This group taps how you make decisions. Successful police officers are sensitive to unspoken messages, can detect and respond to other people's feelings, and make fair and accurate assessments of a situation, rather than being influenced by their own personal biases and needs. Once the decision to act is made, second-guessing can be dangerous. Police officers must make their best judgments in line with accepted practices, and then act upon these judgments without hesitancy or self-doubt. Finally, it's important to know and accept that you cannot change the world single-handedly. People who seek this career because they want to make a dramatic individual difference in human suffering are likely to be frustrated and disappointed.

- A score over 360 indicates you may be trying too hard.
- If you scored between 170 and 360, your style of making decisions, especially about people, fits with the desired police officer profile.
- Scores between 80 and 170 suggest that you think about how you make judgments and how much confidence you have in them.
- If you scored between 80 and 170, making judgments may be a problem area for you.

Group 4—Authority

Add up scores for questions 1, 10, 13, 18, 22, 25, 32, 34, 39, and 45.
TOTAL = 280

This group contains the essential attributes of respect for rules and authority—including the "personal authority" of self-reliance and leadership—and the ability to resolve conflict and work with a team. Once again, a good balance is the key. Police officers must accept and communicate the value of structure and control without being rigid. And even though most decisions are made independently in the field, the authority of the supervisor and the law must be obeyed at all times. Anyone on a personal mission for justice or vengeance will not make a good police officer and is unlikely to make it through the screening process.

- A score between 160 and 360 indicates you have the desired attitude toward authority—both your own and that of your superior officers. Any higher is a bit extreme.
- If you scored between 100 and 160, you might think about whether a demanding leadership role is something you want every day.
- With scores between 0 and 100, ask yourself whether the required combination of structure and independence would be comfortable for you.

Group 5—Style

Add up scores for questions 5, 9, 14, 20, 24, 29, 32, 36, 41, and 49.
TOTAL = 320

This is the personal style dimension, which describes how you come across to others. Moderation rules here as well: Police officers should be seen as strong and capable, but not dramatic or heavy-handed; friendly, but not overly concerned with whether they are liked; patient, but not to the point of losing control of a situation. A good sense of humor is essential, not only in the field but among one's fellow officers. Flexibility is another valuable trait—especially given all the changes that can happen in one shift—but too much flexibility can be perceived as weakness.

- A score between 160 and 360 is optimal. Over 360 is trying too hard.
- Scores between 80 and 160 suggest that you compare your style with the description in the previous paragraph and consider whether anything needs to be modified.
- If you scored between 0 and 80, you might think about the way you interact with others and whether you'd be happy in a job where people are the main focus.

This test was developed by Judith Schlesinger, PhD, a writer and psychologist whose background includes years of working with police officers in psychiatric crisis interventions.

SUMMARY

The Police Officer Suitability Test reflects the fact that being a successful police officer requires moderation rather than extremes. Attitudes that are desirable in reasonable amounts can become a real problem if they are too strong. For example, independence is a necessary trait, but too much of it creates a Dirty Harry type who takes the law into his or her own hands. Going outside accepted police procedure is a bad idea; worse, it can put other people's lives in jeopardy.

As one recruiter said, the ideal police officer is "low key and low maintenance." In fact, there's only one thing you can't have too much of, and that's common sense. With everything else, balance is the key. Keep this in mind as you look at your scores.

CHAPTER four

ALL ABOUT POLICE OFFICER EDUCATION

I was always interested in public service and public safety. Before I went to college, I was a fire department explorer and then a volunteer. In college, I worked with several police and fire agencies. After graduation, I applied to police departments in New York, Boston, Philadelphia, and Chicago. The only one hiring was in Rochester, New York. I had to take the civil service exam, and score well to get hired. In agencies that use the test, your score is the most important part of the process. It doesn't matter what your abilities or education are if you don't score well.

—Chief of Police, 11 years experience

IT MAY not seem that in today's technologically oriented workplace the need for advanced education should be questioned, but this is not the reality in police work. Whether police candidates should have only a high school diploma, a two-year degree, a four-year degree, or military experience continues to be debated within the profession.

Advanced education in fields such as police studies, criminal justice, public administration, or related fields would seem most appropriate for a better understanding of the nature of police work. But many advocates of education for police candidates believe that any major is appropriate. They believe that what an educated officer brings is not information about policing per se, but a broader perspective on life. This includes critical thinking skills that help an officer to exercise discretion wisely and that contribute to an open-minded approach to people whose backgrounds and lives are different from the officer's own.

This echoes the standards set by police agencies. Of those that expect candidates to have education beyond a high school or General Education Diploma (GED), few specify a major field of study. More likely is a minimum number of credits rather than a specific field of study. Examples of the wording of educational requirements include "some college," "60 credits," "a two-year degree," or, least common, "a four-year degree."

Because a college degree is a requirement for such a small percentage of law enforcement agencies, you may be asking yourself whether you should attend college or whether you should worry about completing college if you receive an offer of employment. For some, this will be as important a decision as accepting a job offer. Consider the following: According to the U.S. Census, in 2007, more than 25% of adults over the age of 25 had at least a bachelor's degree.

Professionally, you must keep in mind that although most departments *require* only a high school-level education, actual hiring practices indicate that more than half the applicants you will be competing against have educations beyond the minimum requirements.

JUST THE FACTS

The questions surrounding whether police officers should be college graduates is not new. They were raised in 1917, when August Vollmer, the chief of police in Berkeley, CA, hired only college graduates as police officers. Few departments, though, followed Vollmer's lead.

You should also consider what an education will mean toward promotion opportunities. Many departments that require only high school or a minimum number of college credits for entry require additional education to move up in rank. As more candidates applying for positions presented more than high school education, many departments feared that rookie officers would be supervised by those less educated than they were. To counter this concern, many agencies have instituted a variety of education requirements for promotion. The progression is simple; more credits are required for each rank than for the one below it. For instance, if a high school diploma is required to become a police officer, 30 or 60 credits might be required to take the test to become a sergeant. If 60 credits are required to become a police officer, to be eligible to take the test for sergeant an applicant might need at least 90 credits and an applicant for lieutenant might be required to have a four-year degree. Not all departments follow this exact credit count, but the basic premise is that each higher rank is more educated than the ones below it. The actual formula may differ, but the theory is the same. If you have already attained the higher level of education upon entry, you will not need to rush to meet those requirements later in your career. This can be especially helpful if by then you have started a family or predict that as you get somewhat older and more involved in your career and your community, your time to pursue your education might decrease.

If your long-term goal is to be a chief of police, particularly in a large agency, a campus police department, or one with education requirements, a bachelor's degree has become a virtual requirement even if not so stated. There are exceptions, but the larger the department, the more likely that a candidate for chief of police will also have a graduate or a law degree. Similarly, candidates running for sheriff, particularly of larger, full-service offices, are as likely to stress their education as their policing experience.

JUST THE FACTS

In the late 1960s, the Law Enforcement Education Program (LEEP) began to provide tuition assistance for in-service officers. LEEP, organized somewhat like the GI Bill, was meant to encourage police officers with college experience who had some college credits, to work toward obtaining an associate's degree (generally two years of college, or a total of about 60 credits) or a bachelor's degree (four years of college, generally between 120 and 130 credits). During its operation from 1968 to 1976, LEEP funded hundreds of thousands of police officers who attended college. By 1975, more than 700 community colleges and almost 400 four-year institutions offered programs they believed would appeal to police officers. Today many schools offer degrees or certificates in police studies, criminal justice, or related academic areas.

The majority of federal agencies require a four-year degree for entry. Some are selective enough to hire only those with degrees in specialized fields such as computer science, accounting, or forensics, or who are fluent in a foreign language.

You might also decide at some point that the irregular hours and weekend and night work do not mesh with your lifestyle but you would like to remain in a criminal justice profession. If so, it is likely that you will require a four-year degree to join a probation or parole agency or many specialized government investigative agencies.

Requirements to move up through the ranks may differ from entry standards in your department, or there may be educational standards for acceptance in some specialized sections. If you enter having attained at least two years of college education, it is more likely that you will be prepared to apply for a specialist position or for promotion. If you have a bachelor of arts or science (BA or BS) degree when you enter policing, you will have the luxury of knowing you are prepared for all ranks and can take advantage of any tuition assistance or programs that encourage you to continue your education at the graduate level. This is an important consideration; according to the same report on departments that require some college, more than 30% of departments reported offering either educational incentive pay (higher salary based on years of education) or tuition reimbursement to those attending classes after being hired.

FIELDS OF STUDY

If you have decided that you will need a four- or two-year degree before or during your pursuit of a police officer career, the next step would be to consider what you will study. Many colleges and universities across the country have Criminal Justice degree programs. However, you don't necessarily need to major in one of these programs.

There are many in the field who believe that a well-rounded college education, one that includes courses in accounting, psychology, foreign languages, and courses that will improve your communication and computer skills, makes for the best candidate. You can concentrate your study on any one of these areas and enhance the skills needed for your future career. The Berkeley, CA police department, for example, requires 60 college credits, and specifies that they be in Administration of Justice, Criminology, Police Science, Public Administration, Psychology, Sociology, and/or English.

JUST THE FACTS

College students are expected at some point in their education, generally in the second or third year, to declare what is called a *major*. This can be defined simply as what you are specializing in and the subject matter you will study in your advanced courses.

All colleges require that a student take a certain number of what are called general education courses. These may be similar to subjects you took in high school such as English, math, government, and history. Others, the liberal arts and humanities, will introduce you to fields such as economics, psychology, anthropology, sociology, history, and possibly a foreign language. Within the past decade, a number of colleges have added courses on ethics and on cultural diversity to provide an introduction to living in a diverse society.

If you do decide to get a bachelor's degree in Criminal Justice, you will probably need 33 credits in your major, which might look like this:

Criminal Justice 101	Introduction to Criminal Justice	3 credits
Law 203	Constitutional Law	3 credits
Sociology 203	Criminology	3 credits
Corrections 201	The Law and Institutional Treatment	3 credits
Law 206	The American Judiciary	3 credits
Police Science 201	Police Organization and Administration	3 credits
Statistics 250	Principles and Methods of Statistics	3 credits
Literature 327	Crime and Punishment in Literature	3 credits
Philosophy 321	Police Ethics	3 credits
Police Science 245	Seminar in Community Policing	3 credits
Police Science 401	Seminar in Police Problems	3 credits

For an associate (two-year) degree, majoring in Criminal Justice, you could take courses such as:

CRIJ 1310	Fundamentals of Criminal Law	3 credits
CRIJ 1301	Introduction to Criminal Justice	3 credits
CRIJ 1306	Courts and Criminal Procedure	3 credits
CRIJ 1307	Crime in America	3 credits
CJCR 1307	Correctional Systems and Practices	3 credits
CJSA 2300	Legal Aspects of Law Enforcement	3 credits

For an associate (two-year) degree, majoring in Criminology, your core course work could include:

CRIM 150	Introduction to the Criminal Justice System	3 credits
CRIM 200	Criminology	3 credits
CRIM 201	Institutional and Commercial Security	3 credits
CRIM 210	Introduction to Corrections	3 credits
CRIM 220	Introduction to Law Enforcement	3 credits
CRIM 280	The Law of Criminal Justice	3 credits
CRIM 285	Introduction to Criminalistics	3 credits
CRIM 298	Practicum in Criminal Justice	3 credits

For all degrees, you will probably be required to take the remainder of your credits in courses such as sociology, math, accounting, computers, writing/composition, psychology, government, and philosophy.

Police Studies

A major in what was once called police science but is now more likely to be called police studies is most often designed for students who want to pursue law enforcement careers or for in-service students. Because it is a popular major among in-service students, if you select this major it is very likely that you will interact in the classroom with a large number of experienced officers.

This can be positive and negative. The positive aspects are that you are immersed in the real world of policing through the questions and comments of your classmates. You may learn of job opportunities firsthand from them, and you will most likely receive encouragement in your career choice. A negative aspect is that hearing these experienced officers complain about department policies may dampen your enthusiasm for entering the field. Another negative, particularly if the professor has been a law enforcement professional, may be that you will feel left out of discussions and wonder what the others all know that you are missing. There is no reason, though, to be intimidated by this. The course content is not based only on current-day policing. A police studies major should include courses in police history and in organizational theories and management. Course work will likely also investigate other areas of the criminal justice system, particularly considering how they interact with or are influenced by the police. Since academic and practical applications often differ, you may learn that your in-service classmates bring a narrower perspective to their efforts than you do.

Criminal Justice

Majoring in criminal justice generally will provide you with the chance to look in greater detail than in police studies at the other areas of the criminal justice system. Generally these include local, state, and federal courts; local, state, or federal corrections; and the fields of probation and parole. Placing the police in this broader context will also involve more courses in government and political science.

Because this major is more general than police studies, it may peak your interest to consider careers in the field that you had not previously thought about. Since some of the other criminal justice professions you will learn about require a four-year college degree, you might decide that your education has opened to you areas that at one time seemed beyond your reach. Many of those in the academic community consider the broader base of the criminal justice degree as a stronger preparation for those planning to attend graduate school, perhaps law school or a school of public administration. While this is not a universally accepted viewpoint, there is a strong possibility that a criminal justice program will expose you to at least one social science research methods course, as well as other specialized areas that might not be included in required police studies courses.

Criminal Justice Administration and Planning

Generally not available in two-year colleges, a major in criminal justice administration and planning may be a wise selection for two types of applicants. If you are interested in moving up in rank or working in an administrative position, this degree will help you to see how criminal justice agencies operate on a day-to-day basis. It will provide you with a deeper knowledge of organizational and management theories, as well as an understanding of the planning process.

This major might also be attractive to you if you are interested in a law enforcement career that may not directly involve policing. Many candidates want to be a part of the policing community but are unwilling or unable to make the commitment to attend a police academy and then to work on patrol or on various hours or days of the week. Possibly you already know that a physical condition will make it difficult for you to successfully complete a police department's selection process but you still want to work within law enforcement. Positions in planning, human resources, finance, and a number of areas are filled by civilians in many police and criminal justice agencies. Bringing knowledge of these fields may help you compete for these jobs.

The degree, as its name implies, focuses on planning, policy analysis and implementation, and management theories and practices applied to the criminal justice system. Because it focuses on management issues, this major will also introduce you to theories of leadership and to internal and external ethical issues faced by criminal justice agencies and their employees.

Public Administration

Like the major in criminal justice administration and planning, a major in public administration provides an opportunity to look beyond criminal justice. In this major, course work may focus on decision making and management in all types of public agencies. You will learn how public administration and public management developed and how it differs from private sector management.

It is similar to a major in business administration but focuses on the public sector. The obvious difference between the public and private sectors involves the need to show a profit. But other areas of difference involve the greater likelihood that the public sector will have a civil service- or union-protected workforce and that salaries are determined through collective bargaining. External political issues may play a different role than in private industry administration. Among the topics commonly covered in this major are economic issues and financial and budgetary management, theories of organization and management, and human resource management processes.

Security (or Protection) Management

Security (or protection) management is, like police studies, a degree program that was initially aimed at working professionals who sought a college degree while also preparing for promotional opportunities at their place of employment. Today many students in this major are in-service personnel. Many are mid- or high-ranking officers who are preparing themselves for careers as managers, consultants, or business owners in the private security sector. Until quite recently, the career path into senior level positions in private security was to have worked as a police officer. This is becoming less true today. As the private security industry has matured and moved beyond supervision of uniformed guards, more managers are coming to the field with educational backgrounds in security issues or with professional backgrounds reflecting technical skills.

For this reason, this major is less directly related to policing than many of the others described. But it is a good choice for those who are not sure that the public sector is where they want to work. Generally, requirements for security guards in most parts of the country are low, but that is not true for investigative or administrative positions in private security firms. Many of these, especially the security departments of large corporations, require applicants to have a four-year college degree.

Many of those hoping to be police officers often have a tendency to dismiss private security as a career option. The field, though, is far more complex and more professional than many in policing realize. It is also one of the fastest growing employment areas in the country. In addition to entry-level security officers, the numbers of private investigators, property protection personnel, threat analysis specialists, and those with the knowledge to integrate surveillance and computer systems have increased substantially in the past decades.

After September 11, 2001, many companies expanded their security networks and a large number of public agencies realized the need for specialized personnel other than routine, uniformed security officers. One of the major consumers of private security services is the public sector. Through contracting out for services, local, state, and the federal government rely on private security firms for such activities as testing products, protecting embassies around the world, undertaking physical threat and vulnerability analyses, and securing computer networks against fraud and virus attacks. Since the private security industry is even more fractured than policing and because much of it is only minimally regulated, it is difficult to estimate the size of the industry. Those who have tried, though, estimate that there are about 60,000 private security firms that together employ at least three times more private security practitioners than there are public police. Estimates are that as much as $90 billion is spent annually on private security throughout the United States.

If you are entrepreneurial and have thoughts of someday working in the private sector, this major might be of interest to you. If you select this field you will learn the history and current practices of the security industry, review case studies of successful security programs and analyze security vulnerabilities, and consider programs to reduce losses in public institutions and private corporations.

Forensic Science

A major in forensic science provides academic and professional training for those who want to work in forensic science laboratories as researchers or administrators, or who are planning to pursue careers as research scientists, teachers, or medical professionals.

Although this is one of the fastest growing majors in the country, it is also one of the least understood. Reflecting the influence of television and movies, many students enroll in the major with the belief that it will prepare them to be crime scene investigators. While some law enforcement agencies do employ civilian crime scene investigators, the majority of departments assign these tasks to those who were police officers and who often hold the designation of detective. Forensic science, as its name indicates, is not about going out to crime scenes at midnight and working with police officers; it entails studying science and then working in a laboratory.

If you select this major you will study chemistry (organic, analytical and physical) biology, physics, and law. Full-service state police agencies, statewide investigative bureaus, and many police departments have forensic labs, making this a growing source of employment in criminal justice. The number of private labs that contract with law enforcement agencies has also increased substantially. Juries have come more and more to expect that forensic evidence will be offered in any case that comes to trial. It is not uncommon to read in local newspapers that a jury returned a not guilty verdict based on the absence of forensic evidence, even if other evidence existed.

This is an exciting and growing field, but it is important that you realize that forensic science requires knowledge of science (including physics) and math (including calculus), requires coursework that involves long hours in a lab, and is not a shortcut to becoming a detective or crime scene investigator.

Homeland Security

Since the September 11, 2001 terrorist attacks, more than 200 colleges have created homeland security programs and about 150 others have added programs in emergency management that focus on terrorism-related issues. Not all the programs are two- or four-year degree programs; some offer a four- to six-course (generally 12 to 20 college credits) certificate program. A study in 2005 by the American Association of Community Colleges found that 80% of two-year institutions offered courses in homeland security, although not all offered majors in this area.

Generally, these courses include a historical overview of terrorism and the development of weapons of mass destruction (WMD), the psychology of terrorists, investigation of terrorism incidents and intelligence gathering, and disaster response.

Many of the students in these courses are, like you, interested in careers in law enforcement, intelligence analysis, and investigations, but many are also in-service professionals seeking to expand their skills for work in the private sector. Other areas for which a degree or a certificate in homeland security might be beneficial include threat and vulnerability analysis, strategic planning, threat mitigation, and incident command and emergency management.

Before selecting a college primarily on the basis of a homeland security program, make sure to determine whether it is a degree program or a subspecialty of a larger program. While either may suit your purpose, if you have determined that you prefer a degree-granting program, you do not want to expend funds for a program that is not what you had anticipated.

CHOOSING A SCHOOL

Just as the fields of study for a police career have grown, so has the number and types of schools that offer these degrees. Selecting the college or university that will best suit your needs, likes, and goals means making many decisions, including those about the type of school (community college, two- or four-year institution), overall size of the school, location, and quality of programs. Would you prefer a single-sex or coed environment? Large classes held in lecture halls, or smaller classes in which you get to know your professors? Do you want to go to a local school and live at home, or are you willing to relocate and perhaps live in on-campus housing?

You can explore these options and many others by enlisting the help of experienced high school guidance counselors or career counselors. Keep asking questions—of yourself and them—until you have the information you need to make your decision. If you are not currently in school, use the resources listed in the appendix at the end of this book. And whether in school or not, you should talk with those who are already working in law enforcement about their experiences. Ask where they went to school, what advantages they gained from their education, and what they would do differently if they were starting again.

Keep in mind during your search that there are three types of schools offering college credit. If you are interested in a two-year degree, will live at home, and work while getting your education, you might consider a community college. These are public institutions offering vocational and academic courses both during the day and at night. They typically cost less than both two- and four-year public and private institutions. You will need a high school diploma or GED to get in, and depending on your course of study, you could have one of the following when you are finished:

▶ a certificate
▶ a license
▶ an AA degree (associate of arts)
▶ an AS degree (associate of science)
▶ an AAS degree (associate of applied science)

You can find out where community colleges are located in your area by contacting your state's Department of Education. Or use the Internet to find community colleges, which are usually listed by state.

Junior colleges are two-year institutions that are usually more expensive than community colleges because they tend to be privately owned. You can earn a two-year degree (AA or AS), which can usually be applied to four-year programs at most colleges and universities. Again, use the Internet to help you with your search.

Colleges and universities offer undergraduate (usually four-year) programs in which you can earn a bachelor's (and often master's and doctoral) degree in a variety of fields. Entrance requirements are more stringent than for community colleges; admissions personnel will expect you to have taken certain classes in high school to meet their admission standards. Your high school grade point average (GPA) and standardized test scores (most often the Scholastic Aptitude Test, or SAT) will be considered. If your high school grades are weak or it has been some time since you were last in school, you might want to consider taking courses at a community college to bring you up to speed. You can always apply to the college or university as a transfer student after your academic track record has improved.

JUST THE FACTS

If you live near one of the four-year colleges you are thinking of attending, try to visit during open houses for applying students.

Ask whether the major you are interested in is housed within a fully operational academic department or is a small segment of a larger department. This may impact the number of faculty assigned to teach in the program and whether they are full-time and will be available if you need guidance.

Be aware that state or public colleges and universities are less expensive to attend than private colleges and universities because they receive state funds to offset their operational costs. Tuition for out-of-state students at public colleges may be two or three times what it is for state residents; generally, though, they are still less expensive than private institutions.

Another thing to consider when choosing a college is its placement programs in law enforcement. Does it have a relationship with area law enforcement agencies, in which the agencies actively recruit on campus, and may even use the campus as the site for their law enforcement academies? Attending a school with such a relationship could greatly improve your chances of employment upon graduation.

Are you considering only colleges within commuting distance of where you live? This may limit your search, but may allow you to focus solely on comparing a handful of programs. This may be more helpful than trying to compare schools around the country. As with your job search, the more places you consider, the wider your options—but they may become more confusing. The further from home the college is located, the less likely it is that you will have the opportunity to visit the campus and gain firsthand information about the program, the faculty members, and the general ambiance.

If you already have a two-year degree and are now ready to transfer to a four-year college, inquire as to whether you will receive full credit for your courses at the college of your choice. Many two-year colleges and four-year colleges that are near one another or are part of the same state university system sign what are called articulation agreements. This means that if you obtain an associate's degree from a signatory two-year college, all your course work will be accepted toward your bachelor's degree. You will begin your four-year college career with junior class standing and generally will need only another 60 credits to obtain your degree. If you enroll in a college that does not have an articulation agreement with your community college, you are likely to have to provide documentation on what was covered in your earlier courses and to request transfer credit. With this arrangement, there is no guarantee that each of your courses will be accepted toward your degree program. You may have to take some additional course work, which can be costly and time-consuming. If you are thinking of attending a college that does not have an articulation agreement with your community college, ask whether you can have your courses evaluated for credit before you enroll.

JUST THE FACTS

The following chart gives a few examples of how education can pay off. The numbers in the "Bonus Pay Added to Base" column illustrate how much extra is added to your base salary in return for the number of college hours you earned or the kind of degree you have.

Department	College Hours or Degree	Bonus $ Added to Base (per year)
Albuquerque Police Dept. (NM)	Bachelor	1,620
	Masters	1,920
	PhD	2,200
Atlanta Police Dept. (GA)	Associate	1,379
	Bachelor	2,760
Dallas Police Dept. (TX)	90 hrs	720
	Bachelor	1,200
Indianapolis Police Dept. (IN)	Bachelor	1,000
Lexington Police Dept. (KY)	30 hours	450
	Bachelor	1,500
Orlando Police Dept. (FL)	Associate	360
	Bachelor	960
	Salary incentive courses	up to 1,560

If you will be relocating to attend college, learn about living arrangements. In addition to the different cost of living in different parts of the country, you should learn whether the college of your choice has dormitories for all students or if placement is dependent on distance from the campus. If there is a possibility you will be unable to live in a dormitory because of space limitations, school regulations, or because you will relocating with family members, will the college assist you in any way to obtain off-campus housing? Are there dorms or apartments for married students, students with dependents, students who would prefer to live with a local family than on their own? All of these are questions you need to ask if you are considering moving away from home to attend college.

Four-year institutions also are very likely to expect you to attend the majority of your classes on the colleges' main or auxiliary campuses. The majority of colleges and universities expect you to complete at least one or two years' worth of credits at that institution. Since they are often less concerned with accommodating working students, four-year institutions may offer fewer courses on weekends or online. If you are a local student, this may have minimal impact because you may be living at home and within an easy commute of the institution. If you are not local, this will impact where you live and travel arrangements to the institution.

ONLINE COLLEGES

Some colleges permit enrolled students to take a few courses online, but within the past two decades colleges have developed programs that are totally online. These programs are aimed at students who never attend in the classroom or who might do so only for very short periods of time. In addition to enrolling many students who are interested in policing careers, these all-online institutions enroll many in-service police and military officers who often have little control over their work schedules.

Online colleges are not the same as brick-and-mortar colleges. You need not be a registered student to take courses. Online colleges are defined as those that offer degrees solely online. Some are affiliated with a college with a physical campus but others exist only in cyberspace. Many of the strictly online colleges aggressively market criminal justice degrees. Since the terrorist events of September 11, 2001, many have added degrees or certificate programs in homeland security.

Online education may be convenient, but some institutions charge by credit rather than by semester and the costs may be higher than students anticipate. In addition, online courses often have higher dropout rates than classroom courses, because many students find it difficult to set aside a sufficient amount of time to complete the work when left solely on their own. If you know you have a tendency to put things off if you aren't reminded to do them, online education may not be your best option.

The range of quality of these programs is vast. If you are considering an all-online program, or one that is not affiliated with a bricks-and-mortar college, there are a number of things you should investigate. Learn whether the institution is accredited by an educational association that is recognized by the U.S. Department of Education (DOE). Any institution of higher learning should be accredited either regionally or nationally. Contrary to common expectation, regional accreditation is of higher value to educators than national accreditation. Many agencies will not accept education from nationally accredited institutions, and a nationally accredited undergraduate degree will not help you get into a regionally accredited graduate program.

State universities, smaller institutions, and online colleges are generally accredited by one of six agencies:

Middle States Association of Colleges and Schools
New England Association of Schools and Colleges
North Central Association of Colleges and Schools
Northwest Association of Schools and Colleges
Southern Association of Colleges and Schools
Western Association of Schools and Colleges

If your degree is accredited by one of these associations, it will be accepted anywhere in the country for employment and for at least partial transfer credits between institutions. If a degree is nationally accredited by the DOE but not by one of the six regional associations, it may not be accepted by all employers or you may not receive transfer credits for courses taken. In addition, if you are attending an institution that is not properly accredited, you may have problems obtaining veteran's benefits or state scholar incentive awards—the funds may not be released for attendance at a school that lacks accreditation.

An Internet search for almost any police or criminal justice topic will bring not only information on the topic, but advertisements for the many colleges that offer online degrees in the field. This larger and growing larger number of schools can be overwhelming to an applicant. Appendix D (Additional Resources) briefly describes a few of the schools that are accreditated and maintain a direct or indirect affiliation with a law enforcement association or with a branch of the U.S. armed forces.

Whether you attend an online or a brick-and-mortar campus college, there is an excellent possibility that you need to work during all or part of your time as a student. Colleges understand the needs of today's students, few of whom are able to count on full support from home. A number of work study options, internships, and scholarships may be available to you either through your school, through a law enforcement agency, or through benefits available to all students regardless of their major fields.

WORK STUDY OPTIONS

Going to school while working is a challenge; for you it may also be a necessity. Your first assignment is finding the balance between education and employment. How many course hours can you take on, including time for studying, researching and writing papers, and taking classes, whether in person or online? How many hours do you need to work to meet your expenses? The type of work, the hours required, and traveling time between work, home, and school all factor into the equation.

If you want to work only in a police agency during your education, check whether your agency of choice or your local police department makes use of reserve, auxiliary, or volunteer officers. Some police departments and sheriffs' offices—but rarely state police agencies—have a position called an auxiliary officer, a part-time officer or a reserve officer. The description varies in different parts of the country and from agency to agency. Sometimes the individuals may be volunteers. In other instances, there may be payment for your time. In general, however, these officers work a limited number of hours per week or per month in support of regular fully-sworn officers. Individuals filling these positions may not be interested in full-time employment as police officers, but others have found them useful as a stepping-stone to joining a department or aiding in finding law enforcement work elsewhere. A good recommendation from a local police chief can be very helpful in adjacent departments.

There is also a possibility that a police agency in your area sponsors sporting programs for youths or other activities where police officers work with community members. If you are talented in one of the areas where police are focusing their attention, you might be offered the chance to assist as a sports or reading coach, or to assist in encouraging citizens to participate in the programs. Although these efforts may be without pay, depending on your skills and the time you are able to devote, the department may at some time offer you monetary compensation through a small stipend, help in paying for books, or support for attending seminars to enhance your leadership or skills training. Here again, a good recommendation from the chief or a senior officer with whom you work can pay greater dividends than the small salary or stipend you might earn.

Work study is used to describe two different types of programs. The first, rare in policing, is for people already working. Here your employer has a policy of allowing you to work fewer hours in order to attend college classes or perhaps vocational schools. A variation on this is the employer who will not reduce your working hours for you to attend classes, but will reimburse you for at least part of your school expenses upon successful completion of your class work, or achievement of a certain grade or certain number of credits or some professional certification or recognition.

The second type of work study program is administered through the college or school you may attend. Your school will help you find employment while you are enrolled. These programs are usually administered through the school's financial aid office. Competition for such aid is keen. If you are looking for tuition assistance be sure to inquire about the types of financial aid, including work study programs, when you begin applying for admission.

The most work study assistance comes from the federal government, which makes grants available to approximately 3,400 participating post-secondary schools. The government allows the schools to establish requirements and restrictions involving the Federal Work Study Program funds, but all jobs must pay at least the federal minimum wage. The work may be at the school itself, performing jobs in the library or at residence halls, or perhaps staffing security posts.

Most university and college police departments have positions that are available to work study students. These are not the glamour jobs. It could be routine clerical work processing on-campus parking tickets or logging in physical evidence collected by technical investigators. It might be doing computer data entry for the department, possibly recording crime statistics or helping with taking college identification photos. Somewhat more adventurous might be assisting officers in providing late nights escort services for faculty, students, and guests going to their cars or residences.

The school also partners with local organizations and agencies, including private nonprofit groups and government agencies performing public services. Work study programs are based on financial need and you must maintain a specified level of academic performance to keep your job. At the same time, the work is designed to be related to your field of interest and academic course of study. The number of hours and days you work can vary, based on whether classes are in session or whether it is a vacation period or time between semesters. Many police departments and some sheriffs' offices accommodate work study students with jobs in areas of non-enforcement, such as picking up and delivering documents between headquarters and precincts or performing various clerical duties at headquarters.

JUST THE FACTS

In order to participate in the Federal Work Study Program, and many other types of aid, you must complete the Free Application for Federal Student Aid (FAFSA), which can be done as early as your junior year in high school. The forms are available from guidance counselors and financial assistance advisors. They are also available at the U.S. Department of Education webpage: fafsa.ed.gov. This application is a basic financial assistance document that is used almost universally for many different purposes. Just accurately completing the form is a learning exercise that will serve you well in opening your eyes to the first of many applications you will be asked to complete as you move through education and begin your career path.

It is smart to complete the FAFSA form in the event that you may need some type of tuition aid as your education progresses. DOE's deadline for filing a FAFSA is only six or eight weeks prior to the start of the school year. The individual state deadlines are based on the state in which your school is located, not the state you live in. This is very important, because the state deadlines are much earlier than the federal deadline. Since the funds for assistance are limited and there are many applicants, you should not wait until the deadline to file your application. A number of deadlines must be met, including the application receipt date and, if changes are necessary, the date the form is finally submitted successfully with all necessary corrections.

Work study programs can be what you make of them. Treat the work study opportunity as a chance to earn while you learn and expand your circle of friends, acquaintances, and possible mentors. The program can provide both a high level of learning and real-world work experience, making it part of a positive period in your life. You will also be networking with teachers and supervisors who will offer you guidance and perhaps letters of reference if you choose to pursue higher education or when you are looking for permanent employment. In addition, you may be working with people in the field who know where there are vacancies and who may also provide you with letters of recommendation.

SCHOLARSHIPS AND GRANTS

This money is awarded to students for a wide variety of reasons, including good grades, financial need, future career plans, ancestry, and even hobbies.

Money for scholarships and grants is available for just about every student. Anything from being in the top 10% of your high school graduating class to playing the piano could make you eligible. And while they probably won't be the sole means of financing your college education (most range from a few hundred to a few thousand dollars a year), scholarships and grants should not be overlooked as a source of financing.

JUST THE FACTS

The Pell Grant is designed to assist students with exceptional financial need. In the academic year 2008–2009, six million students received Pell Grants ranging from $431 to $4,731. To determine whether you might fall within the income limits for a Pell Grant, make sure to check online or to ask your campus financial advisor. There is no stigma attached to taking the money if you are eligible. The program exists specifically to help low-income students attend college.

One scholarship that considers ancestry is awarded by The National Organization of Black Law Enforcement Executives (NOBLE). A scholarship is given to a high school senior, male or female, who is African American, has a minimum GPA of 2.5 and is planning to study criminal justice, law, or a related field. Financial need is a consideration. NOBLE's various chapters throughout the country offer about 35 similar scholarships. For further information, write to:

Noble National Office
4609 Pinecrest Office Park Drive, Suite F
Alexandria, VA 22312-1442
703-658-1529

Women going into a career in law enforcement might apply for a scholarship with the National Association of Law Enforcement Executives (www.nawlee.com), while those with a sports background could contact the

NCAA at 913-339-1906 to find out about scholarships and other funding for athletes.

However, the best way to find scholarship and grant money is to use the Internet. You enter the appropriate information about yourself, and a search will take place which will give you a list of those awards for which you are eligible. If you want to expand your search, your high school guidance counselors or college financial aid officers also have plenty of information about available scholarship and grant money.

JUST THE FACTS

Campus-based aid is administered through the school rather than directly by the government. Participating schools are free to set rules, restrictions, and regulations as long as they comply with federal guidelines. In the case of the Federal Work Study Program, the government makes funds available to schools and other organizations, which in turn provide jobs and tuition remission to qualifying students. Other campus-based aid programs include the Federal Supplemental Educational Opportunity Grants (FSEOG) and the Federal Perkins Loan program. FSEOGS are given primarily to students who qualify for Pell Grants, while the Perkins loans are made in the $4,000 to $6,000 range at 5% interest. The basic requirements for these and most federal aid include being a U.S. citizen or eligible non-citizen with a Social Security number. You must also have a high school diploma or a GED.

LOANS

You can get loans that are backed by state and federal dollars to finance your education. Unlike grants and scholarships, they must be paid back with interest. However, interest rates on student loans are usually lower than the rates on any other kind of loan.

Although scholarships and grants, and even work-study programs, can help to offset the costs of higher education, they usually don't give you enough money to pay your way entirely. Most students who can't afford to pay for their entire education rely at least in part on student loans. The largest single source of these loans, and for all money for students, is the federal government. Try these three sites for information about the United States government's programs:

www.fedmoney.org   This site explains everything from the application process (you can actually download the applications you'll need), eligibility requirements, and the different types of loans available.

www.finaid.org   Here, you can find a calculator for figuring out how much money your education will cost (and how much you'll need to borrow), and get instructions for filling out the necessary forms as well as information on the various types of military aid (which are detailed in the next chapter).

www.ed.gov/offices/ OSFAP/students   The Federal Student Financial Aid Homepage. The FAFSA can be filled out and submitted online.

You can also get excellent detailed information about different sources of federal education funding by sending away for a copy of the U.S. Department of Education's publication, *The Student Guide*. Write to:

Federal Student Aid Information Center
P.O. Box 84
Washington, DC 20044
1-800-4FED-AID

JUST THE FACTS

PLUS loans, or Parent Loans, are available only to students who are legal dependents. They are available from private lenders through the Federal Family Education Loan Program (FFEL) and from the DOE through the William D. Ford Federal Direct Loan Program.

Stafford Loans are loans determined by the school. Stafford Loans carry a low interest rate and can be either subsidized or unsubsidized. Subsidized loans have a financial need qualification and do not begin to accrue interest until the repayment schedule begins. Unsubsidized Stafford Loans do not require proof of financial need and interest begins accruing at the time the loan is taken out, but usually at rates that are lower than normal commercial loans.

Loan money is also available from state governments. Below is a list of the agencies responsible for giving out such loans.

ALABAMA
Executive Director
Commission on Higher Education
100 North Union Street
Montgomery, AL 36104-3702
Phone: 334-242-1998
Fax: 334-242-0268

ALASKA
Executive Director
Alaska Commission on Postsecondary
   Education
3030 Vintage Boulevard
Juneau, AK 99801-7109
Phone: 907-465-2962
Fax: 907-465-5316

ARIZONA
Executive Director
Arizona Board of Regents
2020 North Central, Suite 230
Phoenix, AZ 85004
Phone: 602-229-2500
Fax: 602-229-2555

ARKANSAS
Director
Department of Higher Education
114 East Capitol
Little Rock, AR 72201
Phone: 501-324-9300
Fax: 501-324-9308

CALIFORNIA
California Student Aid Commission
P.O. Box 510845
Sacramento, CA 94245-0845
Phone: 916-445-0880
Fax: 916-327-6599

COLORADO
Executive Director
Commission on Higher Education
1300 Broadway, 2nd Floor
Denver, CO 80203
Phone: 303-866-4034
Fax: 303-860-9750

CONNECTICUT

Commissioner of Higher Education

Department of Higher Education

61 Woodland Street

Hartford, CT 06105

Phone: 203-566-5766

Fax: 203-566-7865

DELAWARE

Executive Director

Delaware Higher Education Commission

820 French Street, 4th Floor

Wilmington, DE 19801

Phone: 302-577-3240

Fax: 302-577-6765

DISTRICT OF COLUMBIA

Chief, Office of Postsecondary Ed.

Research and Assistance

2100 M. L. King Jr. Avenue, S.E. #401

Washington, DC 20020

Phone: 202-727-3685

Fax: 202-727-2739

FLORIDA

Executive Director

Postsecondary Education Planning

    Commission

Florida Education Center

Collins Building

Tallahassee, FL 32399-0400

Phone: 904-488-7894

Fax: 904-922-5388

Office of Student Financial Assistance

Room 255, Collins Building

Tallahassee, FL 32399-0400

Phone: 904-488-1034

Fax: 904-488-3612

GEORGIA

Georgia Student Finance Commission

2082 East Exchange Place

Tucker, GA 30084

Phone: 770-414-3200

Fax: 770-414-3163

HAWAII

Hawaii State Postsecondary Education

    Commission

2444 Dole Street

Bachman Hall, Room 209

Honolulu, HI 96822

Phone: 808-956-8213

Fax: 808-956-5156

IDAHO

Executive Director for Higher Education

State Board of Education

P.O. Box 83720

Boise, Idaho 83720-0037

Phone: 208-334-2270

Fax: 208-334-2632

ILLINOIS

Illinois Student Assistance Commission
Executive Offices
500 West Monroe Street, 3rd Floor
Springfield, IL 62704
Phone: 217-782-6767
Fax: 217-524-1858

INDIANA

State Student Assistance Commission of
    Indiana
150 West Market Street, Suite 500
Indianapolis, IN 46204
Phone: 317-232-2350
Fax: 317-232-3260

IOWA

Iowa College Student Aid Commission
200 Tenth Street, 4th Floor
Des Moines, IA 50309
Phone: 515-281-3501
Fax: 515-242-5996

KANSAS

Executive Director, Kansas Board of Regents
700 SW Harrison, Suite 1410
Topeka, KS 66603-3760
Phone: 913-296-3421
Fax: 913-296-0983

KENTUCKY

Kentucky Higher Education Assistance
    Authority
1050 U.S. 127 South
Frankfort, KY 40601
Phone: 502-564-7990
Fax: 502-564-7103

LOUISIANA

Office of Student Financial Assistance,
    Louisiana Student Financial Assistance
    Commission
P.O. Box 91202
Baton Rouge, LA 70821-9202
Phone: 504-922-1011
Fax: 504-922-1089

MAINE

Financial Authority of Maine, Maine
    Education Assistance Division
One Weston Court
State House, Station 119
Augusta, ME 04333
Phone: 207-287-2183
Fax: 207-287-2233 or 628-8208

MARYLAND

Secretary of Higher Education
Maryland Higher Education Commission
16 Francis Street
Annapolis, MD 21401-1781
Phone: 410-974-2971
Fax: 410-974-3513

MASSACHUSETTS

Massachusetts State Scholarship Office

330 Stuart Street

Boston, MA 02116

Phone: 617-727-9420

Fax: 617-727-0667

MICHIGAN

Michigan Higher Education Assistance
    Authority

P.O. Box 30462

Lansing, MI 48909

Phone: 517-373-3394

Fax: 517-335-5984

Michigan Higher Education Student Loan
    Authority

State Department of Education

P.O. Box 30057

Lansing, MI 48909

Phone: 517-373-3662

Fax: 517-335-6699

MINNESOTA

Executive Director

Higher Education Services Office

400 Capital Square Building

550 Cedar Street

St. Paul, MN 55101

Phone: 612-296-9665

Fax: 612-297-8880

MISSISSIPPI

Commissioner

Board of Trustees of State Institutions of
    Higher Learning

3825 Ridgewood Road

Jackson, MS 39211-6453

Phone: 601-982-6611

Fax: 601-364-2862

MISSOURI

Commissioner of Higher Education

Coordinating Board for Higher Education

3515 Amazonas

Jefferson City, MO 65109

Phone: 314-751-2361

Fax: 314-751-6635

MONTANA

Commissioner of Higher Education

Montana University System

2500 Broadway

Helena, MT 59620-3101

Phone: 406-444-6570

Fax: 406-444-1469

NEBRASKA

Coordinating Commission for Postsecondary
    Education

P.O. Box 95005

Lincoln, NE 68509-5005

Phone: 402-471-2847

Fax: 402-471-2886

NEVADA

Nevada Department of Education

700 East 5th Street, Capitol Complex

Carson City, NV 89710

Phone: 702-687-5915

Fax: 702-687-5660

NEW HAMPSHIRE

Executive Director

New Hampshire Postsecondary Education

 Commission

Two Industrial Park Drive

Concord, NH 03301-8512

Phone: 603-271-2555

Fax: 603-271-2696

NEW JERSEY

New Jersey Department of Higher Education

Office of Student Assistance and Information

 Systems

4 Quakerbridge Plaza, CN 540

Trenton, NJ 08625

Phone: 1-800-792-8670 or 609-584-9618

Fax: 609-588-2228

NEW MEXICO

Executive Director

Commission on Higher Education

1068 Cerrillos Road

Santa Fe, NM 87501-4295

Phone: 505-827-7383

Fax: 505-827-7392

NEW YORK

The New York State Higher Education

 Services Corporation

99 Washington Avenue

Albany, NY 12255

Phone: 518-473-0431

Fax: 518-474-2839

NORTH CAROLINA

North Carolina State Education Assistance

 Authority (NCSEAA)

P.O. Box 2688

Chapel Hill, NC 27515-2688

Phone: 919-549-8614

Fax: 919-549-8481

College Foundation, Inc.

P.O. Box 12100

Raleigh, NC 27605

Phone: 919-821-4771

Fax: 919-821-3139

NORTH DAKOTA

Chancellor

North Dakota University System

600 East Boulevard Avenue

Bismarck, ND 58505

Phone: 701-328-2962

Fax: 701-328-2961

OHIO

Chancellor

Ohio Board of Regents

30 East Broad Street, 36th Floor

Columbus, OH 43266-0417

Phone: 614-466-0887

Fax: 614-466-5866

OKLAHOMA

Chancellor

State Regents for Higher Education

500 Education Building

State Capitol Complex

Oklahoma City, OK 73105

Phone: 405-524-9100

Fax: 405-524-9230

OREGON

Oregon State Scholarship Commission

1500 Valley River Drive, Suite 100

Eugene, OR 97401

Phone: 541-687-7400

Fax: 541-687-7419

PENNSYLVANIA

Pennsylvania Higher Education Assistance

Agency

1200 North 7th Street

Harrisburg, PA 17102

Phone: 717-257-2850

Fax: 717-720-3907

RHODE ISLAND

Rhode Island Higher Education Assistance

Authority

560 Jefferson Boulevard

Warwick, RI 02886

Phone: 401-736-1100

Fax: 401-732-3541

SOUTH CAROLINA

South Carolina Higher Education Tuition

Grants Commission

P.O. Box 12159

Columbia, SC 29211

Phone: 803-734-1200

Fax: 803-734-1426

SOUTH DAKOTA

Executive Director

Board of Regents

207 East Capitol Avenue

Pierre, SD 57501-3159

Phone: 605-773-3455

Fax: 605-773-5320

Department of Education and Cultural

Affairs, Office of the Secretary

700 Governors Drive

Pierre, SD 57501-2291

Phone: 605-773-3134

Fax: 605-773-6139

TENNESSEE

Tennessee Student Assistance Corporation

Parkway Towers, Suite 1950

404 James Robertson Parkway

Nashville, TN 37243-0820

Phone: 615-741-1346

Fax: 615-741-6101

TEXAS

Texas Higher Education Coordinating Board

P.O. Box 12788, Capitol Station

Austin, TX 78711

Phone: 512-483-6340

Fax: 483-6420

UTAH

Commissioner of Higher Education

Utah System of Higher Education

3 Triad Center, Suite 550

Salt Lake City, UT 84180-1205

Phone: 801-321-7101

Fax: 801-321-7199

VERMONT

Vermont Student Assistance Corporation

P.O. Box 2000, Champlain Mill

Winooski, VT 05404-2601

Phone: 802-655-9602

Fax: 802-654-3765

VIRGINIA

Director

State Council of Higher Education

101 North 14th Street, 9th Floor

Richmond, VA 23219

Phone: 804-225-2600

Fax: 804-225-2604

WASHINGTON

Executive Director

Higher Education Coordinating Board

917 Lakeridge Way, P.O. Box 43430

Olympia, WA 98504-3430

Phone: 360-753-7800

Fax: 360-753-7808

WEST VIRGINIA

Chancellor

State College System of West Virginia

1018 Kanawha Boulevard, East

Charleston, WV 25301

Phone: 304-558-0699

Fax: 304-558-1011

Chancellor

University of West Virginia System

1018 Kanawha Boulevard, East, Suite 700

Charleston, WV 25301

Phone: 304-558-2736

Fax: 304-558-3264

WISCONSIN

Higher Educational Aids Board

P.O. Box 7885

Madison, WI 53707

Phone: 608-267-2206

Fax: 608-267-2808

WYOMING

The Community College Commission

2020 Carey Avenue, 8th Floor

Cheyenne, WY 82002

Phone: 307-777-7763

Fax: 307-777-6567

STEP

The Student Educational Employment Program, administered by the U.S. Office of Personnel Management, his been streamlined into two separate programs used by various federal agencies as disparate as the Defense Contract Management Agency and the Bureau of Land Management and frequently leads to entry-level jobs. The assistance is available to virtually all levels of students, from those in high school, vocational or technical schools, and students pursuing an associate, baccalaureate, graduate, or professional degree. There are two types of assistance. One is designed to provide temporary employment during the school year or during summer vacations as long as the student remains in school. The second type offers the opportunity to engage in work directly related to your major field of study.

The Student Temporary Employment Program (STEP) must be renewed annually and the work you do is not necessarily related to your academic work. The Student Career Experience Program (SCEP) is a partnership involving the student and the agency. Work duties are designed to relate to your studies, including formal periods of work and study while attending school. This allows you to stay in school, obtain related on-the-job experience, and be paid for the work. It may also lead to permanent employment after you graduate.

The STEP and SCEP programs have similar eligibility requirements. You must be enrolled, or accepted for enrollment, as a degree-seeking student, whether for a diploma, certificate, or another completion document. You must be at least sixteen years old, and be at least a halftime student at an accredited educational institution. The institution can be a high school, a technical or vocational school, a community college, a four-year college or university, or a graduate or professional school. You must maintain a 2.0 grade point average and be a U.S. citizen. Non-citizens may be considered if they are eligible to work in this country under U.S. immigration laws and if no qualified U.S. citizens are available for the position.

THE NATIONAL GUARD

Another approach to work-study programs involves serving with the National Guard. Specifics vary from state to state, but enlisting with the National

Guard can bring an enlistment bonus that can be used toward tuition or paying off an existing student loan. Credits can be earned toward tuition at in-state colleges, career training that qualifies for college credit, and a monthly paycheck. Service with the National Guard is prized by many law enforcement agencies, which will be a plus when you apply for a job.

Be mindful, though, that National Guard units are mobilized for emergencies such as hurricanes, floods, earthquakes, and blizzards. If that happens, your regular routine—including attending classes—may be disrupted. National Guard units have also been deployed overseas, including to Afghanistan and Iraq; some personnel serve as long as a year or 18 months. While this can be a financially and emotionally enriching endeavor, it is not without risks.

CADET PROGRAMS

Cadet programs range from one with the largest police force in the country to smaller programs in towns, cities, and counties all around the country. For example, the City University of New York (CUNY) and some New York area private colleges participate with the New York City Police Department (NYPD) in a program called the NYPD Cadet Corp. Students enrolled at a participating college work part-time for the NYPD, get tuition reimbursement, and, depending on whether they take and pass the entry exam for police officer, may receive some benefits according to when they are called from the civil service list. Similar programs elsewhere offer on-the-job training in non-enforcement areas at police departments and in sheriffs' offices. Some accept applicants who are no longer in school, but are recent graduates.

STILL IN HIGH SCHOOL?

There are also high school programs that provide an early start on the path toward a career in the field. There are many variations to these programs. One example is a shared time program at the Monmouth County Vocational

School Law Enforcement Program in New Jersey. This is a two-year program that permits juniors and seniors in high school to earn credits transferable to two local community colleges. The High School for Law Enforcement and Criminal Justice in Houston, TX, which opened in 1981, offered one of the earliest secondary school curricula devoted to law enforcement. Currently, there are a number of public high schools offering specialized courses of studies in law enforcement, corrections, and the courts. These include, but are not limited to, the Los Angeles Police Academy Magnet Schools, the Law Enforcement Career Academy at Wheeler High School in Valparaiso, IN; the Sandra Day O'Connor Criminal Justice/ Public Service Academy in El Paso, TX; the High School for Law Enforcement and Public Safety in Jamaica, Queens, NY; the Law and Justice Program at Centennial High School in Roswell, GA; Southeast Academy Military and Law Enforcement High School in Cerritos, CA, and the Criminal Justice and Public and Private Security Program operated by the Chautauqua-Cattaraugas Board of Cooperative Education services in upstate New York near Buffalo.

An alternative to magnet or special curriculum high schools are Explorer Posts specializing in law enforcement. The Explorers are open to 14-year-olds who have completed eighth grade or those who are between 15 years old and 21 years old. Explorer programs include areas of emphasis that include career opportunities, life skills, citizenship, character education, and leadership experience. The Explorers' law enforcement specialty program has been endorsed by both the International Association of the Chiefs of Police and the National Sheriff's Association. With a post that is chartered by a local law enforcement agency, Explorers obtain first-hand knowledge of the work these agencies do while providing support for some of the agencies' community outreach programs. A member of the sponsoring police agency serves as Post advisor and the paramilitary structure of the post generally reflects that of the advisor's organization. As part of their community service orientation, Law Enforcement Explorers are permitted to go on patrol (ride-alongs) with officers. Explorers may also engage in search and rescue efforts for lost children and missing persons as well as receive training in such police functions as report writing, domestic dispute resolution, crowd control, hostage negotiations, and weapons training.

INTERNSHIPS

Internships provide a way to gain first-hand knowledge about the workings of law enforcement agencies. Internships can earn high school or college credits. Most college and universities with police studies and criminal justice programs incorporate internships into their course offerings. In addition to providing you with an opportunity to further your education, these programs are very likely to help you make a career decision.

There are two sources of internships. One is directly between you and a police agency. Many, if not most, police and law enforcement agencies provide internships to qualified applicants. The number of internships at any one agency is limited, so the application process will be competitive.

The second source of internships is through your college. As mentioned previously, virtually all colleges with police studies-related majors offer internship courses. Occasionally, specialized internships are available to students in other majors, such as English, communications, behavioral sciences, and physical sciences. In some cases, internship courses are upper-level electives, which means you must be a junior (third-year student) or a senior (fourth-year student). In other cases they are part of the degree requirement. Although undergraduate internships are generally limited to third- or fourth-year students, exceptions are sometimes made for outstanding or especially-qualified students with fewer credit hours completed. Graduate programs may also incorporate field work involving internships. These, too, are sometimes electives and sometimes part of the degree requirements.

How and where internship students are assigned varies from college to college. Generally, your school will have developed a relationship with law enforcement agencies in the vicinity and will assign you to work with one. In other instances, you will be required to find an agency and make the arrangements yourself—with some guidance from your internship advisor—in order to fulfill the course requirements.

Police agencies at all levels of government provide opportunities for interns: town, village, city, county, and state police departments, as well as sheriffs' offices. Many city and state investigative agencies also provide internships, as do some special jurisdiction police agencies and some of the federal law enforcement agencies. Because of the varied nature of special jurisdiction departments, an internship in one of them will have the added benefit of introducing you to such areas as fraud investigation; enforcement of hunting and fishing laws as well as protecting fish and wildlife, natural resources, historic and archaeological sites; environmental protection agencies; parks services and departments that police parks, beaches, campgrounds and other recreational areas. There are also law enforcement agencies dedicated to transportation and campus policing, two of the growing special jurisdiction law enforcement areas.

Requirements vary, but most agencies prefer applicants who are United States citizens and who are at least 18 years old. Some may require a driver's license or that you are able to assure transportation to and from the assigned work location. You may be asked to sign a confidentiality agreement or to submit to fingerprinting or be tested for drug use. There will be background checks for such things as felony criminal convictions, probation, and adult arrest records. Because interns are both attending school and working in the field, most departments prefer applicants who are not otherwise working. Few agencies that provide internships specify residency in a particular city or county. Generally your attendance at the college with which the internship arrangement exists is sufficient.

In considering an internship, you should ask yourself: What do I expect to learn from this? Work with your professor, faculty advisor, and the coordinator or supervisor at the agency where you will be serving your internship to develop a set of learning goals. These are goals you set for yourself, not just program requirements like keeping a journal or writing a final term paper describing the experience and summarizing what you gained from being an intern.

Before you establish your learning goals, you have to evaluate yourself and your situation. This includes estimating how much time you will be spending on your internship and knowing yourself—your personality, your preferences, your strengths, and your weaknesses. Consider how many hours you will be spending at the work site and what the academic requirements of your internship are. Know your skill set, which means what you are good at. Learn about the agency's mandate and the duties you will be asked to perform to help the agency meet its goals. In some tasks you may be able to perform as competently as a rookie police officer, in many more areas you will find out how much you don't know.

Your list of learning goals should be specific rather than general. That is, instead of having a goal "to learn more about being a cop," you could have as a goal "learning the difference in duties between a police officer and the supervising lieutenant," or "how officers interact with members of the community who need assistance or who report crimes." You might want to learn more about the differences between a local and a county police department, or between a police department and a sheriff's office. These are very general goals. Once you have interned for a while, you might make your goals more specific or even more personal, such as learning what you have to do to become a canine officer or a homicide investigator. If you are good with numbers and enjoy math, you may want to pursue fraud examination involving accounting cover-ups.

Being an intern is an active experience. True, there will be a learning curve in the early stages of the internship. There will also be times when you are put in a passive role as a participant-observer. As you grow on the job, though, you will be expected to become a productive part of the team, doing real work in the job at hand.

One example of a highly specialized internship program is with the Federal Bureau of Investigation, which operates the FBI Academy Law Enforcement Communication Unit Internship Program that brings volunteer interns to Quantico, Virginia, where FBI agents are trained. The FBI Academy also provides advanced training for ranking officers and supervisors from police agencies around the world. The FBI Academy Law Enforcement Communication Unit Internship Program is open to students majoring in criminal justice, English, communications, and related areas of study; majors in other areas may also be considered. The internships consist of 12 weeks of working 8 A.M. to 4:30 P.M. assisting communications staff. The communications unit is responsible for training FBI Academy attendees in interviewing and interrogation, developing informants, public speaking, media relations, and writing skills. The unit also produces the *FBI Law Enforcement Bulletin*, a monthly publication featuring articles on current issues in law enforcement written by people working in the field. Interns typically work on preparing summaries of articles, fact-checking, and other jobs related to editing and preparing the articles for publication.

This is just one type of internship program the FBI offers under it FBI Honors Internship Program. Each summer, about 50 students are brought to headquarters in Washington. Most of the students, who must have at least a 3.0 GPA on a 4.0 scale, are going into their senior year in college or have graduated and been accepted into graduate school. The FBI interns assist in administrative and analytical tasks in such areas as application processing; monitoring recruitment and training policies and procedures in personnel resources; reviewing nominations for in-service recognition and special awards for agents; and working in the National Center for the Analysis of Violent Crime (NCAVC).

The FBI programs are highly specific. Most internships offer opportunities to survey the whole array of police activities and operations. In other cases, you may be able to spend your internship taking an in-depth look at a particular law enforcement specialty. This could include everything from recruitment and training to maintenance of records; communications or community outreach programs; criminal investigations or crime lab and property room; preparing cases and courtroom testimony; or surveillance operations. You might also be able to spend most of the internship period with a special unit, such as canine patrol, motorcycle patrol, accident reconstruction, narcotics, arson squad, or emergency response team, to name a few.

It is unlikely you will have an opportunity to answer calls for service with these units because, of course, both the agency and your school are responsible for your safety. But you may have the opportunity to work in the command center of these units and interact regularly with officers assigned to them. If you have a preference for one type of experience or the other, find out during the application process whether you have a choice in assignments or whether the privilege of being considered for an internship is the extent of your choice.

Wherever you perform you internship work, do not expect to do active police work beyond paperwork and observation. In the field, you will be limited primarily to observing what the job entails and how the others perform their duties. More likely you will be providing routine assistance to either sworn officers or civilian employees of the agency. If you violate policies meant to keep you safe and you consistently try to stretch your responsibilities into active police work, you stand a good chance of having your agency request that your school remove you from the program. You are there to learn about policing and, possibly to help the agency with some non-emergency tasks. You are not there to endanger yourself or others by taking chances and engaging in risky behavior.

Internships not only provide real world experience, they also help you develop self-directed learning. Most of your learning up to this point will have been passive—sitting in classrooms listening to lectures, reading books, and perhaps watching a few videos. With a field work internship, you will learn when there is a preferred method of performing a task or addressing a challenge, and when there are multiple approaches to problem solving, each with plusses and minuses. You will be acquiring new knowledge and probably applying some of the knowledge you have already gained.

Most students find at the end of an internship that they have acquired new skills and experienced personal development. Most important as far as career consideration goes, you will have developed an increased sense of professionalism through your first-hand involvement in real-world work.

Now that you've learned something about internships, you need to know how to go about getting one. General information on internships is available primarily from school internships coordinators and from police agency websites. Some agencies that coordinate a number of programs with more than one college might have an agency administrator. Attend seminars, job fairs, and similar events where you can talk to recruiters about internships. Particularly if you are in your senior year and will be looking for full-time employment soon, discuss with a recruiter whether an internship can lead to direct employment or if it carries extra points on a civil service exam. Because special jurisdiction agencies and some city and state investigative agencies are less likely to be covered by civil service regulations, they often have greater flexibility in hiring. In searching for an internship, do not disregard opportunities closer to home. Friends, relatives, and possibly parents of classmates who work in the field are also a good source of information.

Make sure you start early, since the application process has a series of deadlines. In some cases, the package of application materials may have to be completed as early as one year in advance of when you may want to begin your internship. This is also a good time to start lining up people to use for references and to write letters of recommendation on your behalf.

Once you have determined when and where you would like to apply, read the application requirements carefully. Some applications may have to be submitted in paper form only, sometimes parts of the application may be submitted electronically. In some cases, the entire application form may have to be completed online. First and foremost, follow instructions. This might seem to be unnecessary advice, but a major reason internship application forms are rejected is that the instructions were not followed, resulting in incorrect, inaccurate, or omitted information. Even before you begin filling out the application, read it over and over, so you know what information is being requested. After you have completed the form, read it again to make sure you have followed all the instructions. Check your spelling. Have someone else read your application; a second opinion can be helpful. Remember, too, that the experience you gain going over your internship application very, very carefully will help you do the exact same thing when you complete a police job application.

Sometimes the application process includes one or more interviews. Make sure you dress appropriately; a business suit for men and a daytime dress or business pantsuit for women. It is more important to leave a good impression than to show how fashionable and trendy your wardrobe is. After the interview—later the same day and no later than the next day—send a note to the interviewer saying how much you enjoyed the opportunity to be considered for a position. Since you know you will be sending a note and may be asked to remain in contact with the interviewer, be sure to ask for a business card so you have the person's name and title. If no business card is available, ask the person to spell out his or name, ask for the person's title, and write it down so that in your nervousness and enthusiasm you do not forget. It is better to send a handwritten note through regular mail. An e-mail note would not have the same impact, but would be better than sending no thank you note at all. A phone message or a text message is not appropriate, and perhaps would be viewed as intrusive by the interviewer.

SCHOLARSHIPS

There is another way to finance your education that does not entail taking a job or paying back a loan. These are scholarships. As discussed in the work-study section, the Free Application for Federal Student Aid (FAFSA) is the basic document that helps you determine the types of aid for which you are qualified and how much aid you may receive, whether in the form of grants, work-study awards, or loans. At the same time you are working your way through the FAFSA procedures, you should also be looking into scholarships as another way to help you pay your way through school.

Truthfully, there is not much funding from within the law enforcement community for students who are not in-service police officers. That does not mean, though, that your entire education must be financed out of your own pocket. Federal, state, or local police fraternal groups of women and minority officers may have scholarship programs. Although each group may have only a handful of scholarships available, they are generally not well-publicized, so checking with these groups may result in a small amount of funding directly. Many of the professional associations described in Appendix A provide small scholarships to applicants who match their criteria. In addition to the national groups, local chapters may also assist you. Some scholarships are restricted to the children of members; others will consider any applicant with an interest in a law enforcement career. For instance, the National Sheriff's Association's (NSA) scholarship program is open to employees in sheriffs' offices across the country as well as their children. State sheriffs' associations also sponsor scholarships, awarding them to applicants in law enforcement programs and to upper level criminal justice majors.

Even if the group cannot help you directly, a group member may introduce you to local businesspeople or civic associations that will help you either directly with funds or through part-time employment to help defray your costs. If you are the spouse, child, or in any way related to someone currently in law enforcement, you may be eligible for scholarships set aside specifically for this purpose.

Since the creation of the U.S. Department of Homeland Security (DHS), some communities have made scholarship monies available for individuals studying in the fields of law enforcement and public safety. The Police Corp Scholarship Program is a federal effort that provides renewable scholarships toward undergraduate degrees in return for going through Police Corp training and serving four years in at-risk communities after graduation.

You or your parents' employers, union, church, veterans association, ethnic heritage organization, or social group may sponsor scholarships. Some scholarships have an economic need component, but not all do. Others may include an element of academic merit; you may be asked to submit a paper you wrote for class or write an essay specifically as part of the scholarship application.

Whole books are written about the types of scholarships, who sponsors them, and who is eligible, yet no one book covers the subject completely. Schools offering law enforcement-related majors often have listings of scholarship funds available for students pursuing those degrees. There are other guidebooks that list scholarships available through each school. By sorting through these lists, you may be able to come up with schools that could match both your academic preferences and your financial assistance requirements.

For federal tuition assistance, FAFSA functions as a master document; there is no similar centralization in seeking out scholarships. You will have to complete an application form for each scholarship you apply for. Even though much of the information requested on each application is the same, you will have to do each one individually. Some scholarships are available through competitive testing, some are based on where you live, what school you plan to attend, or the high school from which you graduated.

A major part of applying for scholarships, and internships as well, is the resume. The word *resume* is borrowed from French and means *summary*. The resume is a brief outline of who you are and what you have accomplished up to this point in your life. This definition may make it seem that a resume is simple to prepare, but the opposite is true. You should not ramble on about yourself. A resume should be a one-page, at most two-page, document highlighting your education and work experience up to the present. There are websites, library books, and aids that advisors can provide on resume writing. Most will advise you to put your name, address, and contact information at the top. Other information is grouped by topic: educational background, work experience or employment history, outside activities including memberships, personal interests, hobbies and activities, and references. References should be handled in one of two ways. If this is a one-of-a-kind resume intended for a specific person or organization and references were asked for, then you should provide the contact information for those who will recommend you. As a general rule, however, you may also use the phrases "references upon request," so the people you have lined up to speak or write on your behalf are not contacted every time you send your resume with an application. Resumes may get circulated widely; do not include your Social Security number or your personal e-mail address. Since you may at some point be asked for an e-mail address, if yours is in any way in questionable taste or obscure, set up a screen name that is more businesslike. How you choose to present your life and education on your resume is your choice. But remember that a resume is designed to make an employer want to interview you or a donor to offer you money to further your education.

You will most likely need a resume for most of your working life. If you start a good one now, it will need only updating as you complete your education or change your career goals. Other reasons for changes include changes in milestones on the road of life. The most obvious use of a resume is when you are seeking employment, but a resume is a useful document in other areas. It provides a summary of information when applying for a loan or seeking to join a new organization, for example. If you are called upon to speak before an audience or address a group, your resume is a reference tool for the person who has to introduce you and may not know you personally. Now is a good time to start working on a resume you can be proud of and reuse throughout your career.

Just as a resume starts early and builds as your career builds, so should your scholarship search. If you plan on continuing your education after high school, it is never too early to start researching scholarships. The earlier you begin your search, the more likely you are to find sources of support that you did not anticipate.

CHAPTER five

JOB OPPORTUNITIES AT THE LOCAL, STATE, AND FEDERAL LEVEL

Many people want to get into policing without being aware of how people-oriented the job is. Your success as an officer is based on how well you get along with others, so I am looking for this quality from those I interview. I can always teach someone how to fill out a police report; what I can't teach is the human relations side of the work.

I also need officers who are as interested in education as they are in enforcement. It is our duty to be dedicated to crime prevention, which is educational by nature. The police are often called upon to answer questions about home and personal security. We even instruct the public on how to be sure children's car seats are installed properly.

—former Training Coordinator

HUNDREDS OF law enforcement jobs exist at local, state, and federal levels. The number of agencies and the different roles can seem complicated. The time and energy you will invest in learning about your career options can seem overwhelming, but the search is worthwhile. Job satisfaction, salaries, and the level of job security that come with a law enforcement career make it a highly desirable profession. Add to this your good fortune to be considering a career with jobs available throughout the country in all areas of the field.

According to statistics of state and local police agencies compiled by the Bureau of Justice Statistics (BJS), of the more than one million people employed by the almost 18,000 police agencies in the nation, about 732,000 were sworn officers. Local police departments accounted for 61% of the total, followed by sheriffs' offices (24%), state police agencies (8%), and special jurisdiction police agencies (7%).

Between 2000 and 2004, full-time police employment increased by more than 5.5%, representing more than 57,000 new police officers. Some of the increase is due to new homeland security functions that many police agencies undertook after September 11, 2001, but this was not the sole reason. Also, despite a decline in violent crime rates, many agencies grew due to efforts involved with community policing and greater community involvement generally, becoming more involved with forensic analysis, including managing crime laboratories, and assuming responsibilities for sex offender registries and related activities.

In addition to the increased number of police jobs available, information is also more easily obtainable than ever before. In previous years, most applicants did not look far from home unless their interest was in federal law enforcement. Prior to the 1980s, it was common for as many as three-quarters of police applicants to have a family member or friend working in policing, specifically the very department to which they applied. While certainly this can be an advantage, it is no longer accurate today. Women and minority applicants are far less likely to have a relative or friend in policing and all applicants are able to expand their job search through guidebooks like this one and via the Internet. Previously it might have been possible to learn the salary ranges of a department in a particular city or a group of departments in a particular area. Today the Internet makes it possible for you to visit the webpage of any department you might be interested in working for to learn its salary range, selection criteria, and testing schedule if one exists.

This helps account for the changing face of the American police officer. Not only are police officers better educated than the entry level requirements might indicate, there are also more women and minority males in policing than ever before in U.S. history. A look at the new face of policing should encourage you to pursue your dream regardless of your race or sex, height or weight, or whether anyone else in your family and among your friends is already in the field.

As you saw in Chapter 1, women and minorities had a difficult time gaining a foothold in policing and an ever more difficult time winning the right to police equally with majority group males. While white males are still the single largest group of applicants, the playing field for job candidates has leveled.

According to statistics collected by the U.S. government, in the 1960s African-Americans made up only 3.6% of all sworn officers. By the 1970s the figure increased to 6%, rising again in the 1980s to 7.6%, and in 2000 to 11.7%. Increases of Hispanic-Americans were similar; comparable figures are 4.6% in the 1980s, 6.2% in the 1990s, and 8.3% in 2000. Overall, in 2004, racial minorities comprised about 24% of local officers and 19% of deputy sheriffs.

Typical of the changes in policing, in late 2008 the New York City Police Department (NYPD), the nation's largest department, with more than 36,000 officers, reported a 50% increase in the number of Hispanic officers in the ranks up to captain, the highest union-covered rank in the department, and a similar increase in the appointed ranks. While the numbers themselves are not large and do not mirror Hispanics' 28% of the city's population, the 20 Hispanic-American at the ranks of captain and above can be expected to grow as the lower ranks diversify, as is already the experience in the NYPD.

It is more difficult to individually measure other minorities because they are grouped together rather than listed individually, but between 1987 and 2003 the percentage of all other minorities in policing grew from about 1% to about 3.5%. One measure of the new diversity, though, can be seen in the number of departments making scheduling accommodations for Muslims and orthodox Jews whose religious observances often make it difficult, if not impossible, for them to work certain hours or specific days of the year. Some accommodations to uniform regulations have also been made for Sikhs and other groups whose religious or cultural practices bar them from cutting their hair or exposing certain parts of their bodies.

Currently women of all races comprise about 13% of police officers. This is an average; the percentages differ for local policing, state policing, and federal law enforcement. The percentages of women are smallest in state policing. The average of all agencies is only about 5% but larger state agencies tend to have larger percentages of women and highway patrol agencies tend to have the smallest percentages. The percentages of women in federal law enforcement are closer to the average of 13%, but there are considerable differences among agencies.

Another way to chart the changes for each of these groups is not only their total percentages but the rates at which they are being hired. Although the percentages of women being hired has not increased within the past five years, this is because the number of applicants has fallen off. It is not that departments do not want to hire women; it is that women are not applying for the available jobs. This does not mean that if you are a female applicant, you should be discouraged. What others do should not influence you. In fact, since many departments are actively interested in diversifying their workforces, you may discover that you will be actively recruited by a number of departments.

As the figures show, the percentage of minority men in policing has increased substantially. This trend is likely to continue and over time, as older officers retire, police departments will reflect a new racial and ethnic dynamic. This is already apparent is in the number of women and minority men who are moving up the ranks. In some large cities, such as Washington, DC, and Detroit, the majority of senior officers are members of minority groups; the same is true for the Metropolitan Atlanta Rapid Transit Authority (MARTA), the special jurisdiction police department responsible for policing Atlanta's rail and bus transit system. Major cities, small communities, and special jurisdiction police agencies have seen increases in the numbers of women and minority men not only in supervisory and management ranks but in the position of chief of police. The numbers of elected sheriffs who are women or minority men have also increased in all parts of the country, particularly in the south.

Policing as an industry is one of America's major employers and is a major economic engine. In the year 2000, the total operating budgets of the almost 18,000 different police agencies totaled $36,692,534,000. Most of this money was spent on personnel costs, which means the salary and benefits you will be earning as a police officer. Amounts differed based on the size of agencies, but small departments (serving populations up to 25,000) spent between $42,300 and $73,200-plus per officer. Departments serving larger populations spent considerably more—between $83,500 and $90,000 per sworn officer. These larger departments are more likely to be unionized and covered by a collective bargaining agreement (called a union contract) but are also more likely to be in areas with higher costs of living.

Salary is obviously an important consideration in your job search but it should not be your only consideration. Police jobs are available throughout the country and in a variety of types of agencies. If you are interested in relocating to another part of the country, your job search should include agencies in areas in which you might want to live. Obviously, not every candidate is able to consider moving away from home, but if you are able—or even eager—to relocate, you may be successful in using your job search as a catalyst for making a life-changing decision. Remember also that salary indicates the amount of money you will make, not the amount you will spend. The cost of living differs substantially around the country; use the Internet to search for housing and living costs in an area. If you compare salaries and the cost of living in a number of areas, you may decide that the department that pays the highest salary may not actually be the best choice for you.

As you consider the opportunities in the different types of agencies, you should consider what some human resources specialists call a P-E fit, which stands for a person-environment fit. Simply put, this means that candidates are generally attracted to an organization that matches their aims, values, interests, and other aspects of their personalities.

For instance, if you are seeking a family-friendly environment, a job that requires you to be away from home frequently and that has irregular hours and days off may be less appealing to you than a job in an agency that permits you to work steady tours and rarely expects you to travel. Travel is an inherent part of federal law enforcement; you must frequently be away from home and you will be expected to transfer every few years. Other family-friendly policies that may interest you are health benefits not just for you, but also for your dependents. A maternity light-duty or leave policy or a family leave policy that provides time off to care for relatives or for family emergencies might better suit your needs than one that permits such time off only through use of vacation time.

If you like to work outdoors, a special jurisdiction agency that is responsible for parks or recreational areas would likely be a better P-E fit than working as a jail deputy in a local sheriff's office or aiming for a job inside a forensic laboratory where you would mostly be analyzing evidence.

Some of this may seem obvious, but candidates are sometimes so eager to begin a career that they jump at the first offer made to them only to later regret having not waited for the second or third agency they interviewed with. Although today many police agencies are having problems filling vacancies, many police managers were themselves hired when the jobs were scarce and candidates would do almost anything for a position. This means they will rarely give you much time to consider an offer of employment. While they might expect you to say "yes" immediately, it is always wise to try to get at least a few days before accepting an offer. Do a final mental check to consider whether what you have learned up to now is what you had expected.

Taking as much time as you are permitted to before deciding to accept employment is particularly important for police jobs. Make sure your decision is not influenced by television or movies; do you really know what will be expected of you? Since most people remain in policing for an entire career, generally with the department they started in, does the agency provide an environment that seems to fit your needs and goals? If you are close to earning your college degree, would you be wiser to wait until you graduate and then resume your job search? The answers will be different for each applicant.

While no department will give you much time before deciding, remember that saying yes immediately and then changing your mind may affect how you are viewed by another agency. Starting an academy and dropping out early may be seen as a failure on your part rather than just a rash decision. Just as the department will expect you to learn the value of exercising discretion, your first important discretionary action may be deciding that an agency has the P-E fit you are looking for.

LOCAL POLICE DEPARTMENTS

It is not an exaggeration to say that local police departments throughout the United States, regardless of size and area, are recruiting candidates. Numerous articles in police publications have featured police chiefs discussing their cities' problems finding police candidates. At the same time, local newspapers in many parts of the country have highlighted the numbers of vacancies in departments. Some agencies have actually been paying bonuses to current officers who recommend candidates who successfully complete the screening process and graduate from the police academy.

Departments have also begun to actively recruit outside of their geographic areas, often at college campuses with large criminal justice or police studies programs and also at job fairs aimed at various minority communities. Gyms and athletic events have also become active recruitment areas and various programs exist to encourage military veterans to become police officers. A number of departments that require candidates to have completed 60 college credits for employment accept two years of military service with an honorable discharge in place of the college requirement.

Although the job outlook is positive in policing, candidates whose primary interest is local policing often do not understand just how difficult it is to compare police departments to one another. Large city policing is not only different from small town policing in the types of calls an officer might respond to, but also in employment considerations. Here, as in many aspects of policing, television and movies provide an unrealistic picture of the profession, tending to focus on the largest agencies. Of the total number of police departments in the nation, though, the smallest category of agencies is those that employ 1,000 or more full-time officers of all ranks. Fewer than 100 departments employ this number of personnel, while more than 5,000 departments employ fewer than five people.

The few very large municipal departments, including the NYPD and the departments in Chicago, Los Angeles, Detroit, Cleveland, Atlanta, Houston, Dallas, and Newark, NJ, tend to influence overall employment figures disproportionately. Of the 79 departments that in 2004 were among those employing more than 1,000 officers, 20 actually decreased their total staff complements while smaller agencies added personnel. If you live in a major metropolitan area, whether your local police department is growing or shrinking will depend on a number of factors, including past hiring practices, the local economy, whether the city is adding population or is annexing geographic areas adjacent to the city's boundaries, and whether there is a public demand for additional police visibility that local politicians feel they must address.

If you live in a city that has seen a declining population and declining tax base, your municipal department will rarely have increased in size. Conversely, if you live in one of the fast-growing areas of the nation, there is an excellent chance that your local police department has grown in recent years. Following this pattern, many large Midwestern departments, including Detroit and Cleveland, have seen a drop in the number of police officers, while cities such as Las Vegas, Austin, Atlanta, and Albuquerque have seen double-digit percentage increases.

It is likely that many candidates do not live in areas of extreme contraction or extreme growth. You may not live anywhere near either the largest of the smallest agencies or in an area of rapid expansion or contraction. Most likely, your local police department falls somewhere in the middle. It is probably one of the more than 8,000 police departments that employ more than five but fewer than 250 officers. In these departments, learning about job opportunities may be on a more personalized basis than seeing an ad for a civil service test in the newspaper.

If you are in college, taking advantage of a work-study or internship option available through your school that places you in a local police department may be an excellent way to learn about full-time employment opportunities. If you are not a college student, inquire whether your high school has similar programs. If you have graduated from high school but are not attending college, consider becoming active in community groups or even in the police department as a reserve or part-time officer so that you become aware of job openings as well as to develop a positive reputation that may make the difference between being offered a position or finding out after the fact that jobs were available.

Depending on where you live, you might have overlapping local police departments. Maybe you live in a fairly large city, but there is also a county police department in your area. An example of this is Atlanta, where in addition to the Atlanta Police Department, both Cobb and DeKalb counties have full-service police departments. Both also have large sheriffs' offices that present additional employment opportunities, and the transit agency (MARTA) employs close to 300 police officers. Similar situations exist in other areas. The message is that while you may have a first-choice agency, there are many options available. If you are willing to expand your search you will find many choices just as convenient to your home or school as the agency you had your heart set on.

Areas of consideration for those in metropolitan areas that may not be expanding their numbers of employees are county police departments, sheriffs' offices, and campus police departments, which are discussed later in this chapter. Two of the largest county police departments are located in adjoining counties east of New York City (Nassau and Suffolk counties). The Fairfax, VA and Prince Georges, MD county departments are also close to one another even though in different states. Other large county agencies are the Miami-Dade, FL and Baltimore, MD county police departments.

When considering a county police department, remember to check the requirements carefully. You might be surprised to learn that candidates are expected to present credentials in excess of what a city police department sets as its minimum requirements. In keeping with the often higher income and higher education levels of their residents, many county police departments have education requirements for candidates beyond a high school diploma. Additionally, although many may adopt a more service-oriented philosophy than large-city departments, they frequently resemble state police in their expectations of a high level of physical fitness and firm adherence to regulations and military-style courtesies.

If you are looking for a position in a municipal or metropolitan police department, you can find out about the latest job openings in your community by calling your local or state police department's non-emergency number. They may also advertise in local newspapers and online.

Remember, the largest municipal and metropolitan agencies have the most job opportunities. A list of these agencies follows, beginning with the largest, with contact information.

NEW YORK CITY POLICE DEPARTMENT

www.ci.nyc.ny.us/html/nypd/home.html

1 Police Plaza, 14th floor

New York, NY 10038

Phone: 212-374-5410

Full time sworn personnel (OFC:) 38,328

CHICAGO POLICE DEPARTMENT

www.ci.chi.il.us/CommunityPolicing

1121 S. State Street

Cook County

Chicago, IL 60605

Phone: 312-747-5501

OFC: 13,271

LOS ANGELES POLICE DEPARTMENT

www.lapdonline.org/index.htm

150 N. Los Angeles Street

LA County

Los Angeles, CA 90012

Phone: 213-485-3202

OFC: 9,423

PHILADELPHIA POLICE DEPARTMENT

www.phila.gov/departments/police

8th and Race Street, Franklin Square

Philadelphia County

Philadelphia, PA 19106

Phone: 215-686-3280

OFC: 6,782

HOUSTON POLICE DEPARTMENT

www.ci.houston.tx.us/department/police

1200 Travis 16th floor

Harris County

Houston, Texas 77002

Phone: 713-308-1600

OFC: 5,355

DETROIT POLICE DEPARTMENT

www.ci.detroit.mi.us/police

1300 Beaubien Street

Wayne County

Detroit, MI 48226

Phone: 313-596-1800

OFC: 4,070

WASHINGTON DC POLICE DEPARTMENT

www.mpdc.org/English/Recruiting/Police
Officer/htm

300 Indiana Avenue NW, Room 5080

District of Columbia

Washington DC 20001

Phone: 202-727-4218

OFC: 3,618

BALTIMORE POLICE DEPARTMENT

www.ci.baltimore.md.us/government/police/
police1.htm

601 E. Fayette Street

Baltimore, Maryland 21202

Phone: 410-396-2020

OFC: 3,082

NASSAU COUNTY POLICE DEPARTMENT

www.co.nassau/ny.us/police

1490 Franklin Avenue

Mineola, NY 11501

Phone: 516-573-7100

OFC: 2,935

MIAMI-DADE COUNTY POLICE DEPARTMENT

www.mdpd.metro-dade.com

9105 NW 25th Street

Miami, FL 33172

Phone: 305-471-2100

OFC: 2,920

DALLAS POLICE DEPARTMENT

www.ci.dallas.tx.us/dpd

2014 Main Street, Room 506

Dallas County

Dallas, Texas 75201

Phone: 214-670-4407

OFC: 2,817

SUFFOLK COUNTY POLICE DEPARTMENT

www.bern.nais.com/clients/scpd/scpdshp
.shtml

100 Center Drive

Riverhead, NY 11901

Phone: 516-852-2200

OFC: 2,711

PHOENIX POLICE DEPARTMENT

www.ci.phoenix.az.us/POLICE/policidx/html

620 W. Washington Place

Maricopa County

Phoenix, AZ 85003

Phone: 602-262-6151

OFC: 2,428

BOSTON POLICE DEPARTMENT

www.ci.boston.ma.us/police/

1 Schroeder Plaza

Suffolk County

Boston, MA 02120

Phone: 617-343-4200

OFC: 2,190

MILWAUKEE POLICE DEPARTMENT

www.milw-police.org/

749 W. State Street

Milwaukee County

Milwaukee, WI 53201

Phone: 414-935-7302

OFC: 2,151

SAN FRANCISCO POLICE DEPARTMENT

www.ci.sf.ca.us/police/

850 Bryant Street, Suite 525

San Francisco County

San Francisco, CA 94103

Phone: 415-553-1551

OFC: 2,006

SAN DIEGO POLICE DEPARTMENT

www.san-diego.ca.us/police/career
   index/shtml
1401 Broadway
San Diego County
San Diego, CA 92101
Phone: 619-531-2677
OFC: 1,964

SAN ANTONIO POLICE DEPARTMENT

www.ci.sat.tx.us/sapd
214 W. Nueva Street
Bexnar County
San Antonio, TX 78207
Phone: 210-207-7484
OFC: 1,867

CLEVELAND POLICE DEPARTMENT

www.clevelandpd.net
1300 Ontario Street
Cuyahoga County
Cleveland, OH 44113
Phone: 216-623-5005
OFC: 1,798

COLUMBUS POLICE DEPARTMENT

www.megavision.net/police/
120 Marconi Boulevard
Franklin County
Columbus, OH 43215
Phone: 614-645-4600
OFC: 1,726

LAS VEGAS METROPOLITAN POLICE DEPARTMENT

www.lvmp.com
400 E. Stewart Avenue
Clark County
Las Vegas, NV 89010
Phone: 702-795-3111
OFC: 1,709

ISLAND OF OAHU POLICE DEPARTMENT

www.honolulupd.org
801 S. Beretania Street
Honolulu County
Honolulu, HI 96813
Phone: 808-529-3161
OFC: 1,691

ATLANTA POLICE DEPARTMENT

www.atlantapd.org
675 Ponce De Leon Avenue
Fulton County
Atlanta, GA 30308
Phone: 404-817-6900
OFC: 1,612

BALTIMORE COUNTY POLICE DEPARTMENT

www.co.ba.md.us/bacoweb/services/police/
   html/police.htm
401 Dosley
Towson, MD 21204
Phone: 410-887-3151
OFC: 1,608

ST. LOUIS POLICE
DEPARTMENT

www.co.st-louis.mo.us/police

1200 Clark Avenue

St. Louis County

St. Louis, MO 63103

Phone: 314-444-5624

OFC: 1,600

STATE POLICE AGENCIES

Forty-nine states have some type of state police agency; only Hawaii does not. It is ironic that one of the longest running police series on television was also one of the least accurate. From 1968 to 1980, viewers of *Hawaii Five-0* followed the exploits of an elite state police unit that targeted organized crime. Although the show was filmed entirely in Hawaii, the state police unit was fictional.

The other 49 states all have a state police agency, but not all such agencies are the same. There are two basic types of state police agencies—full-service and highway patrol agencies. In these agencies, most officers (generally called troopers in state policing) work primarily in uniform, although both types of agencies have some plainclothes assignments. The third type of state police agency is a state investigative agency in which all officers are assigned to work out of uniform. While the name of the agency often makes plain the jurisdiction of its officers, the name alone may not signify the types of job opportunities that exist.

As of 2004, state police agencies employed about 58,000 full-time sworn personnel, almost 70% of whom were troopers (the entry-level rank). Slightly over 10% were investigators and the remaining almost 20% were supervisory officers. These figures do not include state investigative agencies, but are based solely on either full-service or highway patrol agencies.

Generally, state police agencies have lower percentages of minority men and all women than local police departments and sheriffs' offices. The reasons are complex; some have to do with these groups, particularly women, having a shorter history in this area of law enforcement. Some women are also discouraged by the emphasis on physical skills and fitness. Another reason seems to be the residential training that is conducted primarily in rural portions of the state.

In recent years, state police agencies have made considerable efforts to increase their numbers of women and minority candidates. They are recruiting actively on college campuses, featuring women and minority males on their recruitment teams and on their websites, and generally trying to create a more inviting culture at their academies without diluting their training routines.

Full-Service Agencies

Most state police agencies are categorized as full-service agencies. The largest agencies in this category are also among the oldest, including (in order of size) New York, Pennsylvania, New Jersey, Massachusetts, and Illinois. Virginia and Michigan also have state police agencies that employ more than 1,000 officers.

The reason these agencies are termed full-service is straightforward. They have many duties in addition to patrol. They conduct investigations for their own departments and, often, for small, rural police agencies that lack the technical skills for complex investigations. Full-service agencies also maintain their state's criminal records system (similar to the federal Uniformed Crime Reporting Program [UCR] maintained by the FBI), and operate a forensic lab for their own use and use by departments that do not maintain their own labs. In a number of states, though, the crime lab is operated by the state's investigative agency rather than by the uniformed agency.

This is one example of why it is important to learn the range of duties of the agency you are applying to. Particularly at a time when forensics has become one of the fastest-growing college major fields of study, if this is your particular passion it is important for you to understand not only what the jobs in crime labs entail but also which agencies in your area are responsible for providing forensic or crime scene services.

Full-service agencies also generally have canine, emergency, tactical, and airborne units, to name just a few, that are sometimes scattered throughout the state, for use by the agency; they can be requested by smaller agencies whenever their deployment would be appropriate. These agencies generally operate a police academy primarily for their own recruits but often open supervisory, management, and special skills courses to other departments. The existence of an agency academy means that training assignments may be available at some point in your career.

In full-service agencies, many state troopers also have an opportunity to function like local police officers because these state agencies provide all patrol and investigative services for many unincorporated areas and respond to calls for assistance just as local police do. Some also provide contract policing to a number of small communities. Contract policing, which is also done by some sheriffs' offices, means that a community pays a state police or sheriff's office to assign officers to the community to function as its local police force. In some rural areas, a resident trooper or deputy sheriff may be the only law enforcement officer in the area, functioning not only as the area's police officer but in effect as its chief of police.

In addition, once you are employed by a full-service agency, you will have opportunities to become a specialist in a number of regulatory areas, because in addition to varied patrol assignments, full-service agencies have oversight of numerous state licensing requirements. Some of these include licensing of special jurisdiction police and licensing of professions for which states have mandated fingerprinting or licensing to practice. Depending on the individual states, this might include hairdressing and barbering, racehorse ownership or employment as a jockey, ownership of or employment in an establishment that sells alcohol, and various gambling- and/or lottery-related employment. Obviously, the more areas for which a state police agency is responsible, the greater the opportunities officers have of developing expertise in specialized enforcement fields.

Highway Patrol Agencies

Highway patrol agencies, as their name indicates, have a narrower range of duties than full-service agencies. Although they may have responsibilities other than simply patrol of the state's roadways and accident investigation, their mandates are not as far-reaching as those of the full-service agencies. Most, like full-service agencies, maintain their own training facilities.

Harking back to their histories as parts of public works or motor vehicle licensing departments, they sometimes remain responsible for oversight of highway construction and truck weigh stations on highways, and they may remain involved with testing and licensing of individual drivers, especially those seeking truck, bus, or motorcycle licenses. Probably the best known of these agencies is the California Highway Patrol (CHP), pronounced "CHiPs," partially due to a television show of that name that aired from 1977 to 1983. Among the others are the Florida, North and South Carolina, and Ohio highway patrols.

Indicating how confusing designations in policing can be, despite its more limited jurisdiction than a full-service state police organization, CHP, which was formed in 1929, is the largest state police agency in the nation; of its almost 10,000 employees, about 7,000 are sworn police officers. An agency's size is often not directly related to its salary scale. The NYPD is more than twice as large as the next largest municipal police department but its salary is not among the highest, yet a study in 2008 determined that CHP officers have the highest maximum base pay of all state patrol officers in the nation, including a generous benefits package. The pay is more closely aligned with California police officers and sheriffs' deputies, in part because CHP salaries are determined in conjunction with the average pay rates of five other California law enforcement agencies—the Los Angeles police and sheriffs' departments, and the San Diego, San Francisco, and Oakland police departments. CHP has been actively recruiting women for a number of years. Its webpage contains detailed information on physical agility requirements, the nature of the job itself, and interviews with high-ranking women in the department.

The example of CHP is meant to alert you to many things you must consider as part of a career in state policing. It is very important to learn the roles and responsibilities of the agencies you are considering joining. If your goals tend toward the social service aspects of policing, a highway patrol agency whose primary function is traffic enforcement and accident investigation might not be a good career fit for you. But you should also not make assumptions about salaries and benefits based on an agency's jurisdiction. Some highway patrol agencies, despite possibly providing fewer career options, may provide salaries and benefits comparable to or better than full-service agencies.

Because physical agility plays a much larger role in the hiring and training of state police officers than of most municipal police officers, state police agencies are likely to provide details of their physical requirements on their websites. Candidates interested in this area of policing, particularly those who are not physically fit or do not desire to remain in top physical condition throughout their careers, should review the minimum requirements carefully to determine whether they are willing to make a commitment to the required level of fitness for the next 20 or 25 years.

State Investigative Agencies

A third type of statewide law enforcement agency, which is distinctly different from either the full-service or highway patrol agencies, is investigative agencies. Although they do not exist in all states, where they have been established they are similar to federal investigative agencies.

In most of these agencies, there are no patrol responsibilities. Investigators work in plainclothes (in business attire or in clothing appropriate for their investigation). They are frequently described as state-level equivalents of the Federal Bureau of Investigation (FBI) because of their relatively broad mandates and because they are often under the control of the state's highest ranking legal officer, just as the FBI is under the control of the U.S. Attorney General through the U.S. Department of Justice (DOJ) chain of command.

These agencies typically investigate fraud and mismanagement in government agencies or within private firms doing business with state agencies. Quite often, because of the complex nature of the cases they handle, these agencies require applicants to have a four-year college degree and some accept only those with prior police or investigative experience. If this sort of agency interests you, your internet search should begin using keywords such as *state investigative agencies* or *state bureaus of investigation*.

The agencies, depending on their histories, go by a variety of names; in addition to bureau of investigation (such as in Georgia and Tennessee), in Florida these functions are performed by the Department of Law Enforcement (FLDLE) and in Minnesota by the Department of Public Safety (DPS). In New York State, the Office of the Attorney General employs sworn police investigators who undertake a variety of fraud investigations in conjunction with the legal staff, but many of them have prior experience in policing; unless you have specific skills it may be difficult to gain an entry-level position.

Again indicative of the differing mandates of these agencies, some hire entry-level investigators and provide all basic policing training as well as the specialized skills needed for the types of investigations under the agency's jurisdiction.

Exactly what types of investigations or other functions are assigned to these statewide agencies? In Georgia, for example, the Georgia Bureau of Investigation (GBI) is comprised of an investigative division that responds to requests for assistance from local police to investigate all major crimes and may undertake drug investigations even if not invited to do so. Specialized teams investigate identity theft and there is a bingo-fraud unit. A crisis intervention team is made up of law enforcement officers who work with mental health professionals to respond to situations in which those with mental illness or brain disorders are in crisis, primarily to provide a medical solution rather than incarceration.

GBI also operates the state's crime information center, which provides information to police officers who may have taken someone into custody and need to know if the person is wanted for a crime or has a past record. The information center functions as the statewide crime reporting network. It receives crime and arrest reports from more than 600 law enforcement agencies in the state of Georgia. The other major responsibility of the GBI is to maintain the state's crime lab. These many responsibilities result in a vast array of job titles, from special agent and narcotics agent to crime lab scientist. As with many similar statewide investigative agencies, the GBI requires a minimum of a four-year college degree for most of its positions.

The Tennessee Bureau of Investigation (TBI) is similar. Initially established in 1951 as the plainclothes division of the Department of Safety, in 1980 it became an independent agency. Of its approximately 500 employees, about half are sworn police positions. The FLDLE, with about 2,000 employees, has additional responsibilities for training and certification of the state's many police agencies. Minnesota's DPS, similar to the GBI, also assigns officers to alcohol and gambling enforcement, maintains a gang strike force, and staffs a bureau of criminal apprehension, a missing persons unit, and the state's crime lab.

This summary of only a handful of bureaus provides you with some idea of the wide range of activities of these investigative agencies. Further reflecting the complicated and often overlapping jurisdictions within law enforcement, not all states have this type of an agency. If one does not exist, it is likely that many of the responsibilities are assigned to the full-service uniformed state police department. Further complicating efforts to learn more about state investigative agencies, rather than being categorized as state police, BJS considers them under the category of special jurisdiction agencies. This is because BJS reserves the designation state police for full-service and highway patrol departments.

All three types of state police agencies tend to hire fewer officers than local police departments. Although they have statewide jurisdiction, many state police and highway patrol agencies are not that large; some are comprised of fewer than 200 employees. The investigative bureaus may be larger than the uniformed forces. Because of the prestige often associated with them, they may consider primarily candidates who are already police officers but most hire at least a few new officers as vacancies occur.

All state police agencies have low turnover rates. Few candidates enter state policing casually; most have sought the position for years. In the case of the investigative agencies, many candidates bring technical training or specialized educational background; others come from other areas of law enforcement.

Yet positions exist. There are always some retirements or resignations. In addition, many state police agencies have expanded their activities in recent years to include greater emphasis on combating terrorism and computer-related crimes. Many have also been assigned to provide expanded crime lab services to local agencies. Unless you bring exceptional training or education in these areas, as a rookie officer you will not be assigned to these specialties, but new officers are being hired to replace those on patrol who are assigned to these expanded duties. As you either gain on-the-job experience or continue your education, opportunities in these new areas may well become available to you.

State police traditionally request that you contact the troop or district office nearest to your hometown for recruiting information. You can also check the list of ten of the fastest growing State Departments below.

CALIFORNIA HIGHWAY PATROL
2555 First Avenue
Sacramento, CA 95818
Phone: 916-657-7261

CONNECTICUT STATE POLICE
1111 Country Club Road
Middletown, CT 06457
Phone: 860-685-8230

ILLINOIS STATE HIGHWAY POLICE
201 East Adams
Springfield, IL 62701
Phone: 217-782-6637

KENTUCKY STATE POLICE
Department of Public Safety
919 Versailles Road
Frankfort, KY 40601
Phone: 502-695-6300

NEW JERSEY STATE POLICE
P.O. Box 7068, River Road
West Trenton, NJ 08628
Phone: 609-882-2000

NEW YORK STATE POLICE
Campus, Public Security Building 22
Albany, NY 12226
Phone: 518-457-2180

OHIO STATE HIGHWAY PATROL
660 East Main Street
Columbus, OH 43205
Phone: 614-752-2792

PENNSYLVANIA STATE POLICE
1800 Elmerton Avenue
Harrisburg, PA 17110
Phone: 717-787-6941

TEXAS STATE POLICE
Department of Public Safety
5805 North Lamar Boulevard
Austin, TX 78752
Phone: 512-465-2000

WASHINGTON STATE PATROL
Headquarters Administration Building
Olympia, WA 98504
Phone: 360-753-6540

SHERIFFS' OFFICES

There are about 3,000 sheriffs' offices throughout the United States, in all states except Alaska, Connecticut, and Hawaii. The overwhelming majority of these offices are countywide agencies almost always led by an elected sheriff. A few cities employ sheriffs to provide court security and manage the city jail; some of these are elected but some are appointed by the mayor or city manager. In a few jurisdictions, New York City being a prime example, sheriff's officers are strictly civil enforcement agents, generally carrying out evictions for nonpayment of rent, repossession of property (often motor vehicles) for nonpayment of loans, or for nonpayment of a large number of traffic violations.

The entry-level position in a sheriff's office is rarely called police officer. If you are hired by a sheriff's office, your title will most likely be *deputy sheriff*, commonly shortened simply to *deputy*. This can be confusing to applicants as well as to members of the public, who often interpret deputy to mean a position conveying high rank, such as a deputy director of a private company. In a police department, the title deputy chief conveys the same status as outside law enforcement, namely this person is most often the second-in-command of the department. In a sheriff's office, the person equivalent to the deputy chief is most often called the *undersheriff*. Generally, other ranks are similar to police departments; a first-level supervisor will most likely be called a sergeant, the next rank a lieutenant, and so on until the rank of undersheriff or chief is reached. The undersheriff (or chief) may be someone who has risen through the ranks of the office or may be an appointee selected by the sheriff.

The majority of sheriffs' offices are in suburban or rural counties. Like so much about law enforcement, many who live in large cities form their ideas about sheriffs from movies and television, where they have been portrayed as either bumbling local hicks or racist segregationists during the 1960s civil rights era. Neither could be further from the truth. Most sheriffs have risen through the ranks of their agencies and eventually choose to run for office. Others have had full careers in other areas of policing, and a few have come from non-law enforcement professions. One of the distinguishing factors of sheriffs is that since they are elected, they must convince voters of their abilities to run the office in a legal and fiscally responsible way.

The two largest sheriffs' offices are in highly-urbanized areas—Los Angeles County and Cook County (Chicago and the surrounding area). Other large agencies include Broward County (Fort Lauderdale, FL, and the surrounding area); Harris County (Houston, TX, and the surrounding area); Jacksonville, FL, and Orange, Sacramento, San Bernardino, and Riverside counties in California. Each of these ranks in the 50 largest law enforcement agencies in the country.

Employment in sheriffs' offices increased about 11% between 2000 and 2004, but not all the increase was in sworn officers. Many sheriffs' offices have come to rely on a larger number of civilian employees; sworn positions, though, grew in that period by about 10,000 deputies. Although the vast majority of sheriffs' offices assigned their deputies to patrol and traffic enforcement functions, not all deputies participated in these activities. A total of about 35% of deputies were assigned solely to jail or court operations.

Because the sheriff is elected, the office is seen as much more his or hers than that of police chief. It is for this reason that it is common to see the phrase "sheriff's office" rather than "department," and for the use of the possessive to underline this more personal association. The personal style of the sheriff may be reflected in other ways, too. Particularly in rural areas where the sheriff is often well-known and may have come up through the ranks of the office, the agency may operate more informally than a police department. There may be less focus on physical training for officers and a more casual, community-oriented style of responding to situations may be encouraged. In this type of office, arrests are not a high priority, but providing service to the community is. Not all sheriffs' offices operate in this way; many adhere to the paramilitary style more common in police departments, but are still very likely to reflect the sheriff's personal preferences more than in other types of law enforcement agencies.

This is an important consideration for job applicants. While any one sheriff may not remain in office forever, in a state without term limits a popular sheriff may be reelected for multiple terms. If you are familiar with the sheriff's office in your area and do not find the sheriff or the law enforcement philosophy of the agency to your liking, it would be wise for you to consider alternative career choices. Sheriffs' offices are less likely than municipal or state police departments to be covered by civil service regulations or to be unionized. This may mean that if you find yourself at odds with the incumbent sheriff, you may also find yourself out of a job. It may also mean that if a new sheriff is elected, he or she may replace deputies or ranking officers *at will*, or for any reason, or for no reason other than seeking more loyal employees.

Thus, if you are considering a career in a sheriff's office, you have a number of important things to research and think about. The first is whether you will be comfortable working for the current sheriff. Do not take a position in a sheriff's office in the hope that the sheriff will not run again or will not be reelected. Your preferences may not match those of the voters of the county, who may be pleased with a sheriff who you consider too folksy, not sufficiently law enforcement oriented, or leaning too much in the opposite direction.

Another concern is whether your position will be protected if a new person is elected or appointed if the sheriff who hired you leaves for any reason. You should not rely merely on past practice for career assurance. Although a particular sheriff's office that lacks career protections may never have undergone a large staff turnover with the election of a new sheriff, that does not mean it could never happen. You might decide to consider employment in a department without civil service or union protections, but you want to know in advance if your career might depend solely on elective politics or on the decisions of the sheriff rather than on your own actions and decisions.

An equally important area to learn about is the scope of the office's responsibilities and your own responsibilities. Does the office you are interested in applying to have both jail and patrol functions? You should learn whether the same deputies do both or whether these are separate job titles. In some offices deputies generally begin their careers working in the jail and are then assigned to patrol. But in others, jail deputies and road deputies are separate job titles and you are hired for either one or the other.

If you are looking forward to riding around the streets and roads of the county enforcing the law and interacting regularly with members of the community, you must make sure the agency you join has patrol responsibilities and that the majority of deputies participate in this activity rather than being limited to court security, jail management, and civil enforcement. And if the jobs have different titles, you must make sure you are aware of which job you are being hired for. While a career in a sheriff's office that does no criminal enforcement can be rewarding, it may not be what you have in mind.

To find out about local job openings in the sheriff's department, call your county employment office. You can also read about departments across the country if you log onto the National Sheriffs Association website, www.sheriffs.org.

Check out the fastest-growing sheriff's departments in the country for job opportunities.

LOS ANGELES COUNTY, CA

Los Angeles County Sheriff's Department
www.la-sheriff.org
4700 Ramona Boulevard
Monterey Park, CA 91754
Phone: 323-526-5541
Full-time sworn personnel (OFC): 8,014

COOK COUNTY, IL

Cook County Sheriffs' Office
www.cookcountysheriff.org
118 North Clark, Room 1079
Chicago, IL 60602
Phone: 800-458-1002
OFC: 5,309

SAN DIEGO COUNTY, CA

San Diego Sheriff's Office
www.co.san-diego.ca.us/cnty/cntydepts/
   safety/sheriff
9621 Ridgehaven Court, P.O. Box 429000
San Diego, CA 92142-9000
Phone: 858-974-2222
OFC: 1,700

PALM BEACH COUNTY, FL

Pal Beach Sheriff's Office
www.pbso.org
3228 Gun Club Road
West Palm Beach, FL 33406
Phone: 561-688-3000
OFC: 1,620

RIVERSIDE COUNTY, CA

Riverside Sheriff's Department
www.co.riverside.ca.us/sheriff
7477 Mission Boulevard
Riverside, CA 92509
Phone: 888-564-6773
OFC: 1,357

BEXNAR COUNTY, TX

Bexnar County Sheriff Department
www.co.bexnar.tx.us/sheriff
200 N. Comal
San Antonio, TX 78207
Phone: 210-270-6010
OFC: 1,169

SACRAMENTO COUNTY, CA

Sacramento County Sheriff Department

www.sacsheriff.com

1000 River Walk Way

Carmichael, CA 95608

Phone: 916-875-0085

OFC: 1,155

SAN BERNARDINO COUNTY, CA

San Bernardino Sheriff Department

www.co.san-bernadino.ca.us/sheriff

655 East Third Street

San Bernadino, CA 92415

Phone: 909-387-0658

OFC: 1,149

BROWARD COUNTY, FL

Broward Sheriff's Office

www.sheriff.org

2601 West Broward Boulevard

Ft. Lauderdale, FL 33312

Phone: 954-831-8900

OFC: 1,029

NASSAU COUNTY, NY

Nassau County Police Department

www.geocities.com/CapitolHill/Lobby/9063

1655 Dutch Broadway

Elmont, NY 11003

Phone: 516-573-6500

OFC: 1,004

ORANGE COUNTY, FL

Orange County Sheriff's Office, Human Resources Department

www.magicnet.net/ocso

2450 W. 33rd Street

Orlando, FL 32839

Phone: 407-836-4070

OFC: 980

HILLSBOROUGH COUNTY, FL

Hillsborough County Sheriff's Office

www.hcso.tampa.fl.us

P.O. Box 3371

Tampa, FL 33601

Phone: 813-247-8000

OFC: 937

ORLEANS PARISH, LA

Orleans Parish Criminal Sheriff's Office

www.opcso.org

2614 Tulane Avenue

New Orleans, LA 70119

Phone: 504-827-6777

OFC: 800

WAYNE COUNTY, MI

Wayne County Sheriff and Airport Police Local 502

www.local502.com

20926 Schoolcraft

Detroit, MI 48223

Phone: 313-534-2307

OFC: 800

SUFFOLK COUNTY, NY

Suffolk County Sheriff's Department

www.co.suffolk.ny.us/sheriff

100 Center Drive

Riverhead, NY 11901

Phone: 516-852-2200

OFC: 764

PINELLAS COUNTY, FL

Office of the Sheriff, Personnel Department

www.co.pinellas.fl.us/sheriff/pcso.htm

10750 Ulmerton Road

Largo, FL 33778

Phone: 727-582-6208

OFC: 698

HAMILTON COUNTY, OH

Hamilton County Sheriff's Office

www.hcso.org

Justice Center

1000 Sycamore Street

Cincinnati, OH 45202-1340

Phone: 513-946-6400

OFC: 764

E. BATON ROUGE PARISH, LA

East Baton Rouge Sheriff's Office

www.ebrso.org

P.O. Box 3277

Baton Rouge, LA 70821

Phone: 225-389-5000

OFC: 625

VENTURA COUNTY, CA

Ventura County Sheriff Department

www.vcsd.org

800 S. Victoria Avenue

Ventura, CA 93009

Phone: 805-654-2311

OFC: 706

CONSTABLES

The modern roles of constables differ by state and sometimes even within a state. Some continue to be elected. In some states constables are recognized as law enforcement officers; in others they are considered attached to the court system, and in others they are civil code enforcement officers. The largest number of constables is in Texas. In 2004 almost 2,500 full-time deputies worked for about 500 constables' offices; approximately 35% of the deputies were assigned to patrol. As with sheriffs' offices, candidates who are considering positions as constables should learn the role the office has within their state and should determine whether it is a career position or one to which deputies are appointed and may be removed at will.

SPECIAL JURISDICTION LAW ENFORCEMENT AGENCIES

Special jurisdiction policing has grown substantially in the last 20 years and from all estimates it will continue to grow. According to figures compiled by BJS, in 2004 almost 50,000 full-time sworn law enforcement officers were employed by the almost 1,500 special jurisdiction agencies that participated in the report. Other names by which these departments are known include special-purpose police, special district police, or special enforcement police.

Each of these phrases is meant to describe police officers whose primary jurisdictions are public buildings and facilities, including colleges, hospitals, and public schools; transportation systems; natural resources and parks and recreation; alcohol, drug, and gambling enforcement; and fire marshals and arson investigators. Many public facilities are protected by private security officers or publicly funded officers who do not possess police authority, but a very large number of public or partially publicly funded entities are authorized to hire police officers with powers identical to or very similar to local police. In some instances, these officers may be limited to exercising their police authority only on the property of or in cases connected to their employers, but in some states their powers are identical to those of local police officers and may actually extend across more than one municipality, or even more than one state.

The list of these types of agencies is vast. It is likely that no matter how unusual your interests, there is an agency dedicated to providing law enforcement services to it.

One of the fastest-growing categories of special jurisdiction law enforcement is campus policing. Campus policing also seems to be attracting large numbers of women and minority male applicants to its ranks, possibly because colleges themselves are seen as actively working to achieve both a diverse student population and a diverse workforce. Transportation policing is also growing. As more cities throughout the nation, particularly in the western and southwestern portions of the country, build transit systems to combat traffic problems, pollution, and urban sprawl, many are upgrading existing security departments into full-service police agencies. A number of cities are also creating new police agencies to take over these responsibilities from local police or sheriffs' offices that have provided service on a contract basis or through creation of small, transit-specific units within the departments. Airports also, many of which have depended on sheriffs' deputies or local police to provide patrol services, are creating airport-specific police departments. Because of the number of opportunities in these areas, each is discussed individually.

Campus Police Departments

Campus police departments are the largest single category of special jurisdiction law enforcement agencies. Despite their growth, though, not all campus agencies are police departments. Ninety percent of public institutions employ sworn officers, while fewer than 50% of private institutions do. Size of the institution also plays a role. More than three-fourths of agencies on campuses with more than 2,500 students are state-certified law enforcement agencies. Estimates vary, but campus police agencies counted by BJS employ about 11,000 full-time officers. Most individual agencies are not large, but within the last decade the ratio of officers to students has increased slightly around the country. Part of the increased hiring has resulted from the number of campuses that have increased their use of sworn police officers rather than security officers.

JUST THE FACTS

Campus policing dates its existence to 1894, when Yale University hired two officers to patrol its campus, which was and still is located within the city of New Haven, CT. This set the pattern of campus policing for more than 50 years. Colleges primarily hired a combination of officers who lacked police authority or officers who had retired from the local police force of the city in which the campus was located. Most of these security departments lacked prestige; they were generally grouped under plant and properties, along with maintenance personnel. As the use of automobiles expanded and students and faculty began to drive to school, parking enforcement became the major responsibility for most of these early campus security agencies.

Changes in status and responsibilities began in the 1970s and have continued since then. The first changes were in response to student activism that led to protests and demonstrations on campuses, resulting in a need for enhanced security coverage. Additional responsibilities were also assigned to campus agencies in response to the expansion of higher education. As campuses grew, along with the vast increase in the number of students, colleges began to realize they needed to also expand their security capabilities. Some private colleges petitioned their state legislatures for permission to appoint fully-sworn police officers. One of the first was Rice University in Houston, TX, which helped to set a pattern of converting its security force into a police force. There was considerable cost in doing this because all officers now had to meet state-mandated background and training requirements.

Another impetus for change occurred when Congress enacted the Crime Awareness and Campus Security Act of 1990. This required all institutions of higher learning to make available to students and the public annual crime statistics and to have available a comprehensive plan for student safety. This, and a series of later laws, led to a greater focus on campus safety at the same time that statistics indicated a rise in crime on campuses.

To address these problems and to allay fears of students and their parents about campus safety, many colleges have upgraded their security forces into full-service police departments, with armed officers. Campus officers have often attended state-certified police training programs and their departments began to resemble local police departments, with canine units, bicycle patrol, and crime prevention and community policing units. In the 1990s, campuses such as the University of Illinois at Urbana-Champaign, Ohio State University, and two University of California branches (Berkeley and Davis) developed their own Special Weapons and Tactical (SWAT) teams rather than rely on local police departments.

Today SWAT teams, canine, bomb disposal, and other high-profile police specialties are common, particularly on the main campuses of large state institutions. Many campuses are located in small communities, though. The population on campus is often larger than the town population. The campus is often a major focal point for cultural and sporting events. The university is often also the largest single employer in the area. And today it is also not uncommon for the campus police department to be bigger, better trained, and better paid than the local police.

Reflecting these changes, the majority of agencies have changed their names from security department to police department to reflect their broader mandate. Many have also widened the jurisdiction of their officers.

Almost 50% of campus agencies refer to themselves as police departments and another 25% use the title of department of public safety, which often indicates that officers are also responsible for safety programs, crime prevention, and providing emergency medical services on campus. As campuses have spread beyond the college gates to include off-campus residence halls, fraternity and sorority houses, and a variety of classroom and lab buildings, many colleges now obtain statewide policing authority for their officers so that they are able to take responsibility for events both on and off campus.

Campus police departments vary considerably in size, which is not re-lated to levels of authority. The largest number of campus officers, almost 350, work for New York University, and all are nonsworn personnel. A 2004–2005 survey of campus agencies by BJS counted 10 with staffs of be-tween 76 and 166 fully sworn police officers. Indicating that they relied on a combination of sworn and nonsworn officers, some campuses with the largest number of sworn police officers were also listed among the largest employers of security staff. Generally, where a mixed force existed, nonsworn officers were assigned to building security and parking-related duties. With some exceptions, colleges that relied on the largest number of police officers tended to be in urban areas.

Because they work within a highly educated community, more than 25% of campus police agencies require candidates to have a college degree or some college credits to match the education level of the community being served. This is considerably higher than for all other areas of law enforce-ment except federal policing. Since many colleges and university extend free or reduced price tuition benefits to all full-time employees and their de-pendents (generally defined as spouses and children), if you were hoping to continue your education while working you may find campus policing an at-tractive alternative you had not previously considered.

If you are currently studying on a campus with its own police department, a good way to learn about positions is to schedule an appointment with the chief or deputy chief. Many of these departments are not required to hire un-der civil service regulations. Vacancies may often be filled less formally than those in a local police department. Due to the large number of agencies, as with other areas of policing, it is difficult to make across-the-board general-izations, but there are indications that campus police departments rely to a greater extent on interviews and background investigations of candidates than on physical agility. This is not to imply that patrolling a college campus is so different from patrolling a small community, but it seems to reflect a greater interest in an officer's overall ability to feel comfortable with a more service-oriented rather than a crime fighter's view of the police role.

As campus agencies have begun to more closely resemble other types of police departments, they have increased their emphasis on employing full-time officers. Despite this, many agencies employ students as part-time officers or for dispatching, parking enforcement, or night-hour student escort services. You might be eligible for a work-study position or for a paid part-time job that can help you to pay for your education. If you are interested in a career in campus policing, either of these options may pave the way for a full-time position once you complete your degree requirements and graduate.

Transportation Agency Policing

Another large category of special jurisdiction policing is related to transportation. About 9,000 police officers are employed by 130 agencies, most protecting airports, but also mass transit systems, maritime ports, and bridges and tunnels. This area of policing has grown and is very likely to continue to grow due to concerns over passenger safety, particularly since transportation networks have been targets of terrorist activity in many countries around the world.

Travelers tend to think of a transit hub, whether an airport, train station or bus depot, bridge, tunnel, or ship or ferry terminal, as a transient place, one that people travel through as quickly as possible and return to only rarely. But this is not at all what these facilities are like. Many, including the largest airports and train stations, are quite literally like cities. There may be thousands of employees who arrive and depart daily. There are also hundreds of thousands—maybe more—passengers, some of whom are regular commuters who park their cars, eat their meals, and do their shopping on the way to or from work, and, particularly in the case of train and bus facilities, pass through on their way from one part of a community to another.

For all these people, the special jurisdiction police are the same as their local police during their time in the facility. Become the victim of a crime and the transportation agency police will take the report and investigate the crime. Have your luggage stolen or your car taken from the parking facility and the transportation agency police will take the report and investigate the crime.

In addition to protecting people, transportation jurisdiction police are also involved in property protection. The infrastructure itself is a potential target. Railcars and tracks, buses, stations and garages, ships and cargo storage areas, airplanes and runways, and bridges and tunnels, for example, all require protection from unauthorized persons. In addition to the obvious terrorist threats, more routine dangers exist due to the potential for accidents in these areas.

Although many transportation agencies assign a larger percentage of their officers to patrol than some large city agencies, transportation police, like local, state, and campus police, often work with canines, especially explosive detection dogs. Many agencies assign plainclothes specialists to counteract the thieves, pickpockets, fraudsters, and scam artists who are attracted to these facilities. Generally, people who are in a rush may not notice they have been a victim of a crime until hours later, which makes them easy crime targets.

JUST THE FACTS

Transportation policing is even older than campus policing. Private railroads established their own police forces as early as the 1840s, when their construction sites were subject to many instances of theft and trespassing. As railroads began to crisscross the country, they discovered an absence of police presence. Because individual police departments developed only as areas urbanized, once the railroads left a particular city's limits, the trains; their passengers, employees, and freight; and the rails and depots were all easy targets for thieves. Train robberies are a staple of many movies depicting crime in the western United States, but they occurred throughout the nation. Less exciting for moviegoers, thefts from rail yards and storage areas were more frequent and a constant problem.

Private railroads continue to employ police officers, but because their hiring processes differ considerably from public agency police and because individual officers may be responsible for large areas that cross state boundaries, the employment opportunities they present are not detailed here. If you live in an area with considerable railroad presence or a city where a railroad is headquartered or maintains a large regional hub, you will likely be able to learn about railroad police from the railroad in your area.

When job candidates think of rail policing today, they are more likely to have in mind urban transit systems, many of which are comprised of both bus and rail. Although not nearly as old as railroad policing, transit policing began officially in 1933 with New York City's subway special police. As early as the 1850s, though, street car operators in a number of cities complained about passengers who were intoxicated or smoking, refused to pay their fares, or preyed upon women, children, and elderly riders. In response, cities began to assign police officers to work on the transit system, sometimes irregularly and sometimes as a regular work duty. Some transit systems hired security guards. As with many special jurisdiction law enforcement agencies, managers and patrons eventually found these arrangements unsatisfactory and full-service police departments were created and staffed to meet the specialized needs of transit systems.

Today's Transit Police

The two largest transportation agency police departments are located in the New York-New Jersey-Connecticut metropolitan area. Both have two-state jurisdiction. The Port Authority of New York and New Jersey Police Department (PAPD) employs almost 1,700 officers, all of whom are recognized as police in both states. Officers may work at any of three major international airports (Newark Liberty, John F. Kennedy, or LaGuardia), smaller airports, the bus terminals in New York City, on the Port Authority Trans-Hudson (PATH) rail line, or the four area interstate bridges and tunnels. The other large, bistate agency is the 650-officer Metropolitan Transportation Authority (MTA) police, many of whose officers work in New York City's Pennsylvania Station and Grand Central Terminal, but some of whom work at smaller facilities in New York and Connecticut. Both agencies offer salaries and benefits that are comparable with area police departments but are less well-known than municipal police departments in their areas.

Two cities in Texas—Dallas and Houston—also employ police officers for their transit systems. Like the PAPD and the MTA police, these officers are employed directly by either Dallas Area Rapid Transit (DART) or the Houston Metropolitan Transit Authority (METRO). Houston's METRO transit officers have an unusual combined jurisdiction of the transit system and the highway network. Other cities, including Washington, DC, Boston, and Atlanta also have independent transit police departments.

Many transit systems developed their own police agencies in part due to the long history of private sector railroads employing their own police, but there is also a practical reason. Many of these systems travel across city, county, and even state lines, requiring police officers to have police authority wherever the trains or buses travel. For instance, officers of the Metropolitan Area Transit Authority (WMATA) in Washington, DC are also recognized by the states of Virginia and Maryland.

Antiterrorist concerns have led a number of smaller transportation agencies, particularly newer, commuter rail lines, to consider upgrading their security departments into police agencies. If you see uniformed officers working on your local transit system, it would benefit you to learn who employs them. Some might be members of the local police department who are assigned to a transit unit and some might be employees of private security companies hired to patrol agency facilities, but some are very likely to be members of the agency's own police force.

Today's Airport Police

Airport police departments developed later but similarly to transit systems. A common development pattern was that local police officers were assigned to an airport and at some point the police department and airport authority decided this was no longer appropriate. The second pattern involved security officers employed by the airport being upgraded to or replaced by fully sworn police officers.

In 2004, almost 100 airports had their own police departments; they employed about 3,000 officers. At most airports, these officers work in conjunction with city or county police or sheriffs' deputies and, since the creation of the Department of Homeland Security (DHS), with Transportation Security Administration (TSA) inspectors. Although their numbers make them highly visible at airports, TSA inspectors are not police officers and must rely on police assigned to the airport if a law is violated.

Rules that require travelers to spend more time at airports have led to a greater focus on policing these facilities. Other than the PAPD, which is not solely an airport police department and is larger than all other transportation police agencies, the four largest airport departments are at the Los Angeles, Washington, DC, Wayne County (Detroit), and Dallas-Fort Worth airports. The Los Angeles Airport Police, with more than 1,000 employees, about half of whom are police officers, is the fourth largest law enforcement agency in Los Angeles County.

Although it is often the largest international airports that have their own police, Rhode Island Airport and the Boise, ID, airport are among the smaller ones with independent police departments. Because of the added responsibilities airport patrol has meant for local departments, a number of cities, including Cleveland, were considering the creation of an airport police department in 2008 rather than continuing to rely on the city police for this service.

A number of airport police departments, like transit police, particularly since September 11, 2001, have added canine units to their patrol forces and have added bicycle patrol of parking lots and outlying areas to increase their visibility and increase their interaction with travelers and employees. Some, including those at Minneapolis-St. Paul (MN) Airport and the Baton Rouge (LA) Metropolitan Airport, are also trained as firefighters and emergency responders, making these jobs particularly sought after by candidates who have fire or emergency medical technician (EMT) training.

Learning about Transit Positions

These agencies are less likely to publicize their police departments than local jurisdictions are. Although a few agencies will list open positions on police-oriented websites or advertise in police-related publications, learning about these jobs from people already in them is often the best route for information. Look closely at the police officers at a transportation facility near you. If the officer's uniform or police patch is different from that of local officers, stop the officer and inquire about his or her agency and jurisdiction. You may be surprised at how much you can learn.

If you have an airport or transit system in your area, you might also check the agency's website for information on its law enforcement arrangements and whether jobs are available. Friends or family members who work in these industries are also a good source of information. If you are a transit equipment fan and are a member of any tour or photo groups, you may also learn about jobs from other people in the group. If your school sponsors work-study options, remember to ask whether these agencies participate. If not and this is an area of interest to you, consider asking the work-study advisor or counselor to include these agencies in the program.

Parks, Recreation, and National Resource Protection

A third category of special jurisdiction policing includes parks, recreation, and national resource protection. According to BJS, there were more than 200 such agencies in 2004, an increase of 26 over the 2000 profile, employing almost 15,000 police officers. The three largest categories of agencies were fish and wildlife, parks and recreation areas, and natural resources protection, which together employed about 12,000 of the total. An additional 3,000 officers enforced waterway, boating, and water resource laws, environmental and sanitation laws, and forest resources. While these numbers may seem small in comparison to the total number of municipal police officers, this category is solely for state and local agencies; it does not include the large number of federal officers working in national parks and other federal government-operated outdoor facilities.

Like their federal counterparts, many of the officers in these agencies enforce myriad laws. Laws pertaining to boating, fishing, hunting, vehicles in protected areas, use of natural resources, protecting historic sites, and related areas are too numerous to count. Some examples of the duties of some of these agencies may give you some idea of the areas of enforcement you could become involved with. The Missouri State Water Patrol, for instance, is responsible for law enforcement and boating safety on the state's rivers and lakes. Officers are also trained to conduct safety programs as well as in rescue and recovery during floods. Their responsibilities are quite different from New York City's Bureau of Water Supply police, who are tasked to police the city's 21 reservoirs, most of which are located beyond the city's boundaries.

Many of these agencies will be covered by local or state civil service regulations. This will make the positions somewhat easier for you to locate than those of campuses, transit systems, and airports. If you live in a large city, these agencies may not advertise locally. Check their websites, your state's website, or the website of a newspaper located in the state capitol, where announcements of these positions may be more likely to appear. If you participate in any of the activities overseen by these agencies you may already know about them or have had contact with their officers.

If these jobs seem interesting to you, follow the same path as described for transit agencies. Ask officers you see about the jobs and how you might apply. Ask civilian employees of the agencies if a policing arm exists. Ask friends and relatives and college advisors what they know about these agencies.

Other Special Jurisdictions (Hospitals and School Districts)

Some special jurisdiction law enforcement agencies do not fall into the broad categories discussed. The first step in seeking employment in these agencies is to know that they exist.

Many hospitals, particularly public hospitals or those affiliated with a major university, have their own police departments. In addition to regular patrol duties, these officers may have special responsibilities for checking and controlling inventory of controlled substances that are routinely stored in medical facilities.

A number of school districts have their own police. These are separate from campus police agencies and are generally responsible for patrolling and responding to incidents in primary, middle, and high schools.

Although opportunities exist in these areas, you should consider your own personality before making serious inquires about employment. If you get depressed or queasy around sick people and people in crisis, or feel faint at the smell of some medications, hospital policing may not be the best choice for you. Similarly, if you do not like children or will be uncomfortable working with educators, social workers, and parents, being a police officer for a school district may not be a good fit for you.

CRIMINAL INVESTIGATIONS AND
SPECIAL ENFORCEMENT AGENCIES

Another category of special jurisdiction agencies are labeled criminal investigations. There are about 100 agencies in this group, many of which are statewide investigative agencies that are discussed as part of state policing. In addition to states, some cities have somewhat similar agencies. They might be called departments of investigation or offices of inspector general. In some states, county prosecutors' offices also have their own staffs of officers who undertake independent investigations or work with local police officers on cases that cross town boundaries. Because these officers are often responsible for complex white collar or fraud investigations, positions may be open only to experienced officers. Yet many of these agencies participate in college work-study programs and if you are assigned to one of them and show special interests or abilities you may be offered a position.

The work of some of these criminal investigations agencies overlaps the last category of special jurisdiction agencies. Termed special enforcement by BJS, these agencies enforce laws relating to alcohol, gaming (gambling) and horse or dog racetracks, drug enforcement that is not handled by another agency, and agricultural law enforcement. Like the work of investigators in the prosecutors' offices, some of the oversight offices' work is highly technical. Although some of the agencies hire entry-level officers, you should learn whether there will be openings for inexperienced investigators or whether the majority of the staff is made up of former police officers who gained expertise in these areas while working in general policing agencies.

In considering employment in a special jurisdiction police agency, you should consider the wide range of duties of these departments and the differing hiring standards of many of them. As indicated, some hire only experienced personnel, often retirees from local police agencies, while some hire those new to the field of policing.

Unlike municipal police departments, though, where duties will be similar regardless of the size of department, the duties of special jurisdiction officers are far-reaching and may differ widely from one jurisdiction to another even when agencies have similar names. Since each agency may present a different job challenge, one of the most important considerations is whether the jurisdiction of the agency is of interest to you. The examples pertaining to hospitals and schools were obvious; however, all special jurisdiction policing involves learning about the laws pertaining to the special jurisdiction as well as quite a bit about the work the civilians in these agencies do. If you have no interest in trains, buses, planes, boats, forests, parks, gambling, or other areas covered by special jurisdiction police agencies you might soon become discontent with the work. In these instances it would have been wiser to await a position in a more general-purpose police department.

TRIBAL POLICE

Tribal police are a unique segment of law enforcement. Because Native-American tribes are separate nations, many tribes maintain a separate criminal justice system on their reservations, including their own police departments. Some of these departments are administered directly by the tribes, others by the Bureau of Indian Affairs (BIA) within the U.S. Department of the Interior. Although there are more than 300 Native American reservations throughout the United States, most located in the western states, only about 200 of them operate their own police agencies. Of these, fewer than 10 have more than 50 full-time officers. Many of the agencies give total or partial preference to Native-American candidates. For this reason, except for candidates in the western United States where some of the larger tribal police agencies are located, candidates interested in policing careers who are not Native-American may find few opportunities for employment in these agencies.

FEDERAL LAW ENFORCEMENT

Despite the media attention to federal law enforcement agencies, they employ a surprisingly small number of people. The federal government employs slightly over 100,000 people who are authorized to make arrests and carry firearms. Obviously, these special agents and uniformed officers are spread across the nation. Of this number, about 1,500 people work in U.S. territories, most in Puerto Rico, and a small number are assigned to foreign countries. The number of federal law enforcement officers had been growing prior to September 11, 2001, but an even more rapid expansion took place after that.

There are many things to learn for job candidates seeking federal positions. Although the FBI may be the best-known federal law enforcement agency, it is not the largest. That distinction belongs to U.S. Customs and Border Protection (CBP), which in 2004 employed slightly fewer than 28,000 officers. Even as the largest federal police agency, CBP employs about 10,000 officers less than the NYPD but about 16,000 more than the FBI.

Also unknown by many job candidates, there are almost 70 federal law enforcement agencies. Not all agencies hire at the same time or follow the same procedures for accepting applicants. Additionally, jobs are not equally spread around the country. Generally, if you are hired by a federal agency, your first assignment will not be in the same city or state from which you were recruited. Where will you go? Much depends on the agency you have joined but also on where the positions are located. About half of all federal officers in 2004 worked in only five locations. In order of the number of officers assigned, those work locations were Texas, California, the District of Columbia, New York (the entire state, but most are in the city), and Florida. If you live in either New Hampshire or Delaware and take a federal job hoping to eventually get back home, your chances will be limited. Each state had fewer than 125 officers assigned, and some federal agencies assigned no officers at all to either one.

You might also consider how narrowly you want to limit your job search. Most candidates for federal policing are interested in positions as special agents, but federal agencies also employ large numbers of uniformed police officers. Generally, the special agent position is classified as GS-1811, which consists of criminal investigation titles. A variety of other job classifications are used for other positions.

If you are interested only in a GS-1811 position, you may be eliminating from consideration a number of interesting jobs, some of which may be more readily available than special agent positions. A large number of the uniformed positions, many of which are in the Washington, DC metropolitan area, give hiring preference to residents of the area. Many of the uniformed positions involve less moving around to various locations. You may be able to spend most or all of your career without the frequent transfers that special agents are expected to make, particularly if they hope to move up to supervisory ranks.

Another important consideration is the possibility of transfer either to a GS-1811 position within the agency in which you are working or to another federal law enforcement agency. Many federal law enforcement positions are advertised internally before they are made known to outside applicants. This means that you may have a better opportunity for an agent position if you are already working for the federal government than you would as an outsider. In addition to this built-in advantage, in many instances the time you have already put in working for the federal government may add to your pension and other benefits and may count toward the number of years you must work before you are eligible to retire at a full pension.

Police job applicants are young and retirement seems very far away, but it is important to remember that 20 or 25 years in a job can begin to seem like a long time sooner than you think, and if you are intending, as are most police candidates, to make law enforcement you life's work, the years of seniority you accrued before moving to the agency you always dreamed of may seem like a blessing many years later.

The majority of those employed as special agents and related titles work for agencies administered by one of four cabinet-level departments—the Department of Homeland Security (DHS), the Department of Justice (DOJ), the Department of the Treasury, and the Department of the Interior. Candidates should be aware, though, that just about all the federal departments have a law enforcement component under their organizational umbrella.

If you are interested in learning about agencies not discussed in this book, a visit to the website of each cabinet-level department will, after a few mouse clicks, take you to the law enforcement agencies under that department. Smaller agencies can be found in the same way; this is an easy way to explore some of the less well-known federal law enforcement agencies.

Remember that less well-known does not always mean smaller. There are agencies with large groups of law enforcers that may be unfamiliar to you but may present employment opportunities. Particularly if you have unique skills or interests, you might be very pleasantly surprised to learn that there is an agency that is an excellent match for you. Additionally, as in many facets of life, the best-known agencies tend to attract the highest number of applicants. While each applicant believes that he or she will withstand any and all competition, the agency that is a perfect fit for you may also be one that is most actively seeking job candidates.

Since its creation in November 2002, the DHS houses the largest number of federal law enforcement personnel. In addition to CBP, agents and officers in the Immigration and Naturalization Service (INS), U.S. Border Patrol, and the Secret Service, as well as the Federal Protective Service and the Animal and Plant Health Inspection Service work within DHS. The Border Patrol is one of the fastest-growing federal law enforcement agencies. If you are able to consider working in one of the southwestern states that share a border with Mexico, and you meet federal hiring requirements, you should learn more about the Border Patrol. Largely unknown to many, the Secret Service has a large uniformed division, many of whose officers work in the Washington, DC area.

DOJ agencies include the FBI, although the largest DOJ agency is actually the Federal Bureau of Prisons, which in 2004 employed more than 15,000 correction officers, a 6% increase over two years earlier. Although corrections positions are not discussed in this volume, this is a growing area of federal employment. Other DOJ agencies are better known, including the Drug Enforcement Administration (DEA), the Marshals Service, and the Bureau of Alcohol, Tobacco, Firearms and Explosives (ATF).

A relatively unknown enforcement arm of the Department of the Treasury is the Internal Revenue Service criminal investigation division (IRS CID), which was created in 1919 to investigate violations of the income tax laws. Despite its relative obscurity, the agency is large; in 2004 it contained almost 3,000 special agents, and had the largest percentage of female agents (30%) of all the traditional federal law enforcement agencies. Among its best-known cases was the conviction of Al Capone for income tax evasion in 1932. In addition to financial investigations involving domestic and foreign currency transactions to the federal government, agents also are involved in enforcing gambling tax laws, fictitious tax refund claims, and aspects of the pornography industry.

A discussion of the largest federal law enforcement agencies cannot begin to capture the diversity of assignments that exist. Many federal agencies are similar to special jurisdiction agencies by virtue of their focused mandates. Working for the Bureau of Land Management or the National Marine Fisheries Service, for instance, will be unlike working for the Secret Service or CBP. The laws enforced will be closer to those associated with parks, recreation, and national resource protection. Similarly, officers working in Veteran's Health Administration medical centers will have responsibilities much like those of officers working in private or public local or state hospitals.

Offices of Inspector General

The last major expansion of federal law enforcement prior to the creation of DHS occurred in the 1978, with the creation of Offices of Inspector General (generally abbreviated as either OIGs or IGs).

OIGs employed more than 3,000 special agents in 2006, but they are little known to job candidates. This is because the OIGs work in all federal bureaus and probably because many of the individual OIGs are not as large as the better-known federal law enforcement agencies.

Not solely law enforcement agencies since they also conduct non-criminal audits of their parent agencies and their contractors, each OIG has a criminal investigative function. Their roots are in the U.S. Army's Office of Inspector General, which was formed in 1778. It was not until the 1960s, though, that government leaders saw a need for such oversight of civilian agencies. After a number of scandals involving politicians, outside consultants, and a number of wealthy businesspeople resulted in prison sentences for many of the participants, the OIGs were created.

By 2006 there were almost 60 OIGs. The largest, that of the Department of Health and Human Services (HHS), in 2003 employed more than 1,600 special agents. Most were assigned to investigating Medicare, Medicaid, and other healthcare program fraud. Similarly, special agents in the U.S. Department of Agriculture OIG are responsible for investigation of fraud in the nation's food stamp program and from farm subsidy programs.

OIG agents in the Department of Housing and Urban Development (HUD) investigate individual and large-scale fraud in the Section 8 housing program, which provides subsidies to landlords who house tenants receiving federal rent assistance. They have also become involved in major drug prosecutions of dealers who operate on the property of government-funded public housing developments.

Another group of agents who range from white-collar to violent crime investigations are those in the Department of Labor (DOL), who, in addition to investigating fraud within such DOL programs as workers' compensation, disability insurance, and pension and welfare programs, also become involved in labor racketeering cases that may involve attempts by organized crime to infiltrate or exercise influence over labor unions.

LEARNING WHERE THE JOBS ARE

The best advice for any job seeker is the following:

Learn the marketplace; find out about all the agencies and their mandates.

Learn where the opportunities are; find out which agencies are in growth areas. What is of concern to the public today will most likely translate into budget authority to hire officers to confront that problem in the near future.

Learn the agency's requirements; do not take for granted what others have told you or what you think is true.

Be flexible; do not have your heart set on only one agency—that will blind you to opportunities that are staring you in the face.

If you follow these general rules and you meet the selection standards for most agencies, you will be well on your way to a long and successful law enforcement career.

Appendix A

Professional Associations

THE NUMBER of law enforcement professional associations is huge. Some are actually unions which bargain collectively for all the officers in a department; others are fraternal or sororal associations for officers of similar race, sex, ethnicity, or religious affiliation. Some associations concentrate on officers with similar types of assignments, such as canine officers, bomb technicians, or training officers. Still other associations are aimed at management ranks, but often permit lower-ranking officers to belong as non-voting members and attend meetings and training conferences.

The list that follows describes some of the larger law enforcement associations. In addition to the groups listed, a more general Internet search using such phrases as "police organizations," "African-American police," "women police," and "sheriffs' associations" will yield hundreds of other groups whose websites can help a police candidate learn more about the profession.

Most law enforcement professional associations are open only to those already employed in the field. However, through these associations, you will find general information about the law enforcement profession, an indication of the range of groups that exist, and, in some cases, advice for applicants, sometimes including links to departments with vacant positions. Additionally, since many of these groups list individual chapters located around the United States, you may be able to establish a relationship with a group in your geographic area that will help you locate a job vacancy or even prepare you to meet the eligibility requirements.

Remember that a job search is not for the bashful. When you find an association listed that mirrors your interests or is based in your area, use the "Contact Us" or a similar link to ask if you are eligible to attend meetings and whether the group sponsors job fairs or offers scholarships for those interested in a policing career.

Airborne Law Enforcement Association (ALEA)

http://www.alea.org

An association of civilian pilots and technicians, sworn officers, and aircraft and avionics manufacturers. It holds a national conference and provides training material for law enforcement agencies interested in developing airborne units. A police candidate with thoughts about becoming a pilot would be well-advised to visit the ALEA website.

American Federation of State, County, and Municipal Employees (AFSCME)

http://www.afscme.org

A national federation of civil service workers, AFSCME is a union, which as of 2006 represented about 1.4 million police officers in more than 100 affiliate associations that support police officers during contract negotiations.

ASIS International (formerly the American Society for Industrial Security) (ASIS-International)

http://www.asisonline.org

Founded in 1955 to professionalize the security industry, ASIS International currently has over 36,000 members in more than 200 chapters throughout the world, most of whom are in management positions in private security companies, although many public law enforcement officers are also members. Generally chapters meet regularly to listen to a speaker discuss an area where private security and law enforcement overlap or where better cooperation is sought. The association publishes a monthly magazine, *Security Management*; many articles are written by security professionals and provide an overview of issues in the field. A number of chapters have college affiliates and offer scholarships to students studying security or planning to enter law enforcement.

Federal Law Enforcement Officers Association (FLEOA)

http://www.fleoa.org

Founded in 1977, FLEOA in 2008 represented more than 25,000 federal agents from more than 65 law enforcement agencies. As the bargaining agent for federal law enforcement officers, FLEOA focuses its activities on such issues as salary, disability benefits, and the right of retirees to carry their firearms. There are a number of links to federal law enforcement agencies on FLEOA's website.

Fraternal Order of Police (FOP)

http://www.fop.net

Founded in 1915 by two police officers, the FOP acts as a union in many jurisdictions, but in others is solely a social group organized into local and state lodges. In 2008 there were more than 325,000 members in more than 2,000 lodges; about half the unionized law enforcement officers in the United States are represented by an FOP lodge.

Hispanic American Police Command Officers Association (HAPCOA)

http://www.hapcoa.org

Established in California in 1973, HABCOA is the largest and oldest organization of Hispanic-American command officers in criminal justice agencies in the United States and Puerto Rico. More than 1,200 officers employed at all levels of law enforcement are organized through 12 local chapters and a national office located in Virginia; a major goal is to encourage the recruitment, retention, and promotion of Hispanic-Americans in law enforcement.

International Association of Campus Law Enforcement Administrators (IACLEA)

http://www.iaclea.org

From a small conference in 1959, IACLEA has grown into an organization whose membership represents more than 2,000 colleges and universities throughout the world, although most are in the United States and Canada. A bimonthly magazine, *Campus Law Enforcement Journal*, reaches close to 2,000 campus law enforcement administrators and provides an introduction into campus policing issues for applicants considering employment in this growing area of policing.

International Association of Chiefs of Police (IACP)

http://www.theiacp.org

Founded under a somewhat different name in 1893, the IACP is the oldest and largest association of police executives; in 2008 its more than 20,000 members came from about 90 countries. In addition to an annual conference that generally attracts at least 12,000 people, many of whom are chiefs of their agencies, regional conferences are also held around the world to accommodate those who cannot get to the United States or Canada for the annual meeting and to address issues of interest outside North America. The IACP issues policies and standards and tries to be a centralized voice for the approximately 18,000 U.S. police departments. It publishes a monthly magazine, *The Police Chief*; articles are often written by chiefs of police highlighting local solutions to law enforcement issues. The IACP also lobbies the U.S. Congress on police-related issues and provides numerous training programs.

International Association of Women Police (IAWP)

http://iawp.org

Formed in 1956 as the continuation of a much earlier association of women officers, the IAWP is open to men and women but is primarily made up of women police personnel of all ranks in all types of law enforcement. Although international membership has grown in the last two decades, most members are from the United States and Canada. In addition to a quarterly magazine, *Women Police*, the IAWP hosts an annual training conference that features an international police scholarship winner and highlights both general police topics and issues facing and successes of female personnel around the world.

International Brotherhood of Police Officers/SEIU (IBPO)

http://www.ibpo.org

A union that supports its member organizations with a full-time staff of negotiators, labor attorneys, and a political action committee that finances pro-law enforcement, pro-union candidates for political office, and that lobbies in Washington, DC and in a number of state legislatures on behalf of its members.

International Brotherhood of Teamsters (IBT)

http://www.teamster.org

In addition to the many other types of workers it represents, the IBT is the bargaining agent for about 15,000 police officers in slightly over 200 agencies. Like the IUPA, it is affiliated with the AFL-CIO.

International Union of Police Associations/AFL-CIO (IUPA)

http://www.iupa.org

A union for law enforcement, corrections, and related support personnel, IUPA was chartered as a national organization in 1954. In 1966 it expanded to include Canadian police associations, requiring a change of name from National Union of Police Associations to its current international title. In 1979, IUPA became the first law enforcement union chartered by the AFL-CIO. In 2008, IUPA represented more than 100,000 members in more than 350 locals in the United States, Canada, Puerto Rico, and the United States Virgin Islands.

National Association of Asian American Law Enforcement Commanders (NAAALEC)

http://www.naaalec.org.

This is one of the newer ethnic-based commanders' organizations. Formed in 2002 by officers from San Francisco, Los Angeles, Houston, and New York City, the group has expanded rapidly. Its annual training conference is held in conjunction with two other groups, the National Asian Peace Officers' Association (NAPOA) and the Asian Law Enforcement Society

(ALES). In addition to promoting recruitment of Asian-Americans into law enforcement, the group provides scholarship assistance to Asian/Pacific candidates.

National Association of Field Training Officers (NAFTO)

http://www.nafto.org

Formal field training for police officers began in the mid-1960s. Prior to that, officers were sometimes assigned to work for a short period of time with more experienced officers, but little attention was paid to who was selected as a trainer. As field training developed into a formal program of instruction and supervision of rookie officers, trainers formed NAFTO and held their first annual conference in 1992. NAFTO's goals are to further formalize and professionalize the roles of trainers in policing, corrections, and communications (dispatching).

National Association of Police Organizations (NAPO)

http://www.napo.org

Founded in 1978, NAPO is a coalition of more than 2,000 police unions and associations that in 2008 represented more than 230,000 U.S. law enforcement officers, 11,000 retirees, and 100,000 civilian supporters.

National Association of Women Law Enforcement Executives (NAWLEE)

http://www.nawlee.com

Formed in 1995 in recognition of the growing number of women in law enforcement management ranks, NAWLEE has partnered with the IACP in conducting two studies of women in policing and provided mentoring and networking for women in ranks above captain and for those interested in advancing to management ranks. Its annual conference focuses on how management issues affect women, who comprise only about 2% of U.S. chiefs and 1% of sheriffs in 2008.

National Black Police Officers Association (NBPA)

http://www.blackpolice.org

A national consortium of African-American police organizations in the United States, NBPA was formed in 1972 with a focus on education, training, and policy issues centered on improving the relationships between police departments and the minority community; evaluating the effects of police programs within the minority community; working to recruit minority officers; assisting in policy development to eliminate police corruption, brutality, and discrimination; and to educate police officers to perform professionally and compassionately. As of 2004, individual membership was about 35,000, with close to 150 professional and student chapters.

National Latino Peace Officers Association (NLPOA)

http://www.nlpoa.org

Formed in 1972 originally to unite Latino officers in California law enforcement agencies, NLPOA claimed in 2008 to be the largest Latino law enforcement organization in the United States, with members at all ranks and in all types of agencies. The association's major goals include the recruitment and promotion of Latino officers, providing various forms of support for Latino officers during their probation period, assisting members in the promotional process, and encouraging officers to participate in education and training programs within their agencies. NLPOA was involved with lowering height requirements and winning bilingual pay in the California Highway Patrol (CHP) and other California agencies. Many state chapters engage in fund raising to support scholarship programs for those interested in becoming law enforcement officers.

National Native American Law Enforcement Association (NNALEA)

http://www.nnalea.org

Formed in 1993 by Native Americans in a variety of law enforcement agencies, NNALEA promotes recruitment of Native Americans into law enforcement, works to foster cooperation between Native Americans and criminal justice agencies, and assists Native American communities in improving the quality of law enforcement under tribal authority. By mid-2003, the group estimated its membership at more than 700; executive officers must be Native American law enforcement officers. A training conference, publications, and a number of public/private partnerships are intended to recruit and retain Native American officers in tribal and other law enforcement agencies.

National Organization of Black Law Enforcement Executives (NOBLE)
http://www.noblenatl.org

An outgrowth of a conference to address crime problems in urban low-income areas sponsored by the Police Foundation and the Department of Justice's Law Enforcement Assistance Administration (LEAA), NOBLE was formed in 1976 by African-American police chiefs. Its more than 4,300 members throughout the United States were joined in 2002 by a chapter in St. Kitts and Nevis, the first expansion beyond the country. Membership is open to anyone interested in a career in law enforcement. The group participates with other major law enforcement groups in consortia aimed at professionalizing policing and working more closely with minority communities. It sponsors a Youth Initiative that offers leadership workshops and communication skills.

National Sheriffs' Association (NSA)
http://www.sheriffs.org

Primarily dedicated to increasing the professionalism of sheriffs' offices, NSA membership is open members of the law enforcement community and also to civilians and corporations. Formed in 1940, the group has grown to more than 20,000 members, holds an annual training conference attended by many of the more than 3,000 U.S. sheriffs and their families, and publishes the monthly *Sheriff Magazine*. NSA participates with other major law enforcement groups in consortia aimed at professionalizing policing. Because sheriffs are generally elected officials whose responsibilities include civil enforcement, court security, and jail management, NSA has worked to establish partnerships across the criminal justice system, with vendors who provide many of the products required to manage a correctional facility—and with private firms interested in publicizing community crime prevention efforts that most sheriffs are involved with such as Neighborhood Watch, Triad, USAonWatch® and Boris the Burglar®.

National Troopers Coalition (NTC)

http://www.ntctroopers.com

Founded in 1977, the NTC is a national association of state police and highway patrol unions that in 2008 had more than 40,000 members. Although the website displays links to a number of states, the links are not to the police agencies themselves but to the employee unions.

Police Association for College Education (PACE)

http://www.post-association.org

The twofold mission of PACE is to encourage police agencies to set a minimum education level of a four-year college degree for police candidates and to match college graduates interested in police careers with agencies that require a bachelor's degree for employment. Candidates may learn about vacancies by visiting PACE's website. Although a far greater number of non-federal agencies require two-year rather than four-year degrees, PACE concentrates on four-year degree agencies.

Police Executive Research Forum (PERF)

http://www.policeforum.org

Established in 1977 by a dozen large city police chiefs, PERF has become a research arm of policing. In meeting its initial goals of enhancing police capabilities to improve crime control and to encourage debate within policing about police issues, PERF has sponsored studies of workplace violence, police response to people with mental illness and the homeless, and local law enforcement's response to terrorism. Although its membership is no longer limited to large city police chiefs, it is one of the few police organizations that require a member to be a police executive of a department of at least 100 full-time employees or to oversee a jurisdiction of at least 50,000 people and to hold a four-year college degree. Applicants must be approved by current members. Although candidates for law enforcement positions are not eligible for membership, summaries of PERF's research are available on its website and provide an overview of issues that leading police executives believe are among the current concerns of the profession.

Society of Police Futurists International (PFI)

http://www.policefuturists.org

Members include police and private security practitioners, educators, researchers, technology experts, and others interested in professionalizing law enforcement through research that involves long-range planning and forecasting, including predicting personnel needs and changes, technological changes, and societal expectations that may impact on the delivery of police services in the future. Futurists present to police practitioners tools to analyze, forecast, and plan in new ways by undertaking research, sponsoring conferences, and publishing a newsletter.

United States Police Canine Association, Inc. (USPCA)

http://www.uspeak-9.com

Formed in 1971 as a result of the merger of two existing groups, the UPSCA accepts as full members any law enforcement officers who are canine handlers, trainers, or administrators and as associate members civilian trainers and handlers and retired officers. With a membership of about 4,000 in 2003, the USPCA each year holds two week-long competitive meets at which handlers and their dogs vie for various levels of certification and honors. A police candidate with thoughts about becoming a canine handler would be well-advised to visit the USCPA website.

Women in Federal Law Enforcement (WIFLE)

http://www.wifle.com

Originally formed by the U.S. Office of Personnel Management to study the reasons women were not becoming or remaining special agents, in 1999 group leaders separated from agency sponsorship and took the name WIFLE. In addition to providing training for women currently employed in federal law enforcement, WIFLE works to increase the number of women by sponsoring events to support college scholarships and by providing information forums to advise women of federal hiring requirements, benefits, and the tasks federal agents typically perform. Although membership is not open to federal agent candidates, WIFLE's website provides an introduction to federal policing and information on what candidates can expect as applicants, trainees, and agents.

Appendix B

Police Exam and Job Announcements

THIS APPENDIX reproduces a number of actual job announcements that were available in police publications, general publications, or online. These are actual job announcements but the filing periods have expired, and you should *not* contact these agencies about employment based on what you see here. Use these announcements to get an idea of how they are worded and what type of information they provide.

New Jersey State Police

Education

An applicant *must* have (1) a bachelor's degree, signifying completion of the undergraduate curriculum and graduation from an accredited college or university or, (2) alternatively, an associate's degree or have completed 60 college credits from an accredited college or university, plus at least two years of satisfactory employment or, (3) alternatively, have completed 30 college credits from an accredited college or university plus at least two years of active duty military service with an honorable discharge.

Age

Applicants must be at least **21 years old** on the date that the initial application is submitted and **must not** reach **their 35th** birthday prior **to** the graduation **date of their State Police class**.

Citizenship

Only citizens of the United States are eligible for appointment to the New Jersey State Police Academy.

Driver's License

Applicants must have obtained a valid automobile driver's license at the time that background investigations begin.

Background Investigation

Applicants must have a good reputation and be of sound moral character. Factors which are automatic disqualifications for the position of New Jersey State Trooper are listed in the application. An applicant's background will be carefully investigated and the answers which are supplied on the application and written examination, are subject to verification. An applicant who has intentionally made a false statement or practiced, or attempted to practice any deception or fraud in this application, in any examination, interview, application, or in securing eligibility for appointment may be rejected from the process. Any intentional misstatement of fact is reason for disqualification from the selection process, and may be punished by law.

Medical/Psychological Examination

If an offer of appointment as a recruit to the NJSP Academy is tendered to an applicant, it will be conditional upon successful completion of a medical examination and a psychological evaluation. A medical examination will be given during which the ability to perform the essential functions of the position will be evaluated by the Division Physician. Visual acuity must be correctable to 20/30 in both eyes, preferably with soft contact lenses. Each potential recruit will be required to authorize access to all health records. The potential recruit will also be required to provide urine samples for drug testing analysis. If the Division Physician should determine that an applicant is unable to perform the essential functions of the position, the conditional offer of appointment will be withdrawn. A psychological evaluation is also conducted. Applicants who successfully complete this phase may be offered an appointment to the New Jersey State Police Academy.

Physical Qualification Test

The Physical Qualification Test (POT) Battery will consist of the following timed tests: 75 Yard Pursuit Run, Push Ups, Sit Ups, and 1.5 Mile Run. Applicants unable to pass the POT will be disqualified from the current selection process. Please visit the POT link on the New Jersey State Police web site www.njsp.org for a detailed description of each test.

PRIOR TO PARTICIPATING IN THE TRAINING CONTAINED IN THIS COMMUNICATION, YOU SHOULD CONSULT VOUR PHYSICIAN TO ENSURE IT IS SAFE FOR YOU TO ENGAGE IN THE NEW JERSEY STATE POLICE PHYSICAL FITNESS TRAINING REGIMENT.

Selection Process

The selection process is a competitive one consisting of an initial application, physical qualification test, written examination, and background investigation. Upon receipt of a conditional offer of employment, a medical examination and a psychological evaluation will be conducted. Applicants are also required to complete a two-day (consecutive/ overnight) instructional weekend program. Appointment to the Now Jersey State Police Academy is contingent upon a number of factors, including the availability of funded positions and approval by the Superintendent of State Police.

Should you desire further information, contact the **Division of State Police Recruiting Unit at 609.882-2000, extension 2853 & 2961**. Visit our web site at www.njsp.org. New Jersey residency is required upon graduation from the Academy.

THE NEW JERSEY STATE POLICE IS AN EQUAL OPPORTUNITY/AFFIRMATIVE ACTION EMPLOYER

Miami Gardens, FL, Police Department

Property/Evidence Control Custodian II

Deadline: Until filled.

Starting Salary: $37,052 mm. to $46,315 mid./DOQ

Nature of Work: This is a non-sworn, non-exempt, full-time position under general supervision of the Support Services Division. The purpose of the position is to provide support for all areas of the police department. This position is responsible for the labeling, storage, and transportation of all evidence to the crime lab and the maintenance and storage of all department equipment. Performs related work as directed. An employee in this classification will participate and coordinate activities within the Property Unit. This position is not of a routine, clerical or ministerial nature and requires the exercise of independent judgment. The incumbent will assign, review, and participate in the work of employees responsible for performing a variety of technical duties related to the receipt, storage, protection, delivery, release and disposition of property and evidence; to ensure work quality and adherence to established policies and procedures; and to perform the more technical and complex tasks relative to assigned area of responsibility.

Minimum Requirements: High school diploma or GED; supplemented by college level coursework with emphasis in Business Administration, Public Administration, Criminal Justice, or closely related field; Associate's or Bachelor's degree preferred; supplemented by four (4) years previous experience working with the systematic receipt, storage, maintenance, issuance and disposal of various property items. Previous supervisory experience preferred. Must possess and maintain, throughout employment, a valid Florida driver license and satisfactory driving record. Applicants qualifying for employment will be subject to a polygraph examination and an extensive background screening.

Crime Scene Technician

Deadline: Until filled.

Starting Salary: $42,421 mm. to $53,026 mid./DOQ

Nature of Work: This is a non-sworn, non-exempt, full-time position under the general direction of the crime scene investigations supervisor. This multi-faceted position provides support for all areas of the police department. The incumbent is responsible for detecting, collecting, preserving, and transporting evidence from crime scenes. Primarily responsible for processing crime scenes that are investigated by the Miami Gardens Police Department. This position involves a large amount of public contact which requires good communication skills.

Minimum Requirements: High school diploma or GED; supplemented by college level coursework with emphasis in Crime Scene Technology, Criminology, Criminal Justice or closely related field; Associate's or Bachelor's degree preferred. Two (2) years of previous experience in processing of crime scenes, latent print examination or related work required. Completion of formal course in basic fingerprint identification, advanced latent fingerprint identification and administrative advanced fingerprint identification conducted by the FBI preferred. Must possess and maintain, throughout employment, a valid Florida driver license and satisfactory driving record. This position involves irregular shift work and shift rotations necessary to provide services 24 hours a day. Applicants qualifying for employment will be subject to a polygraph examination and an extensive background screening.

CSI Supervisor

Deadline: Until filled.

Starting Salary: $51,967 mm. to $64,958 mid./DOQ

Nature of Work: This is a highly responsible position with the City of Miami Gardens Police Department that involves the supervision, training and scheduling of non-sworn Crime Scene Investigation personnel. The CSI Supervisor will oversee daily operations, assist administrative, purchasing and budgeting functions and perform service calls for the City of Miami Gardens Crime Scene Investigations Unit. The CSI Supervisor supervises staff, delegates assignments, implements field staff work schedules, assists in recruitment/testing/hiring activities, evaluates employees and oversees and provides forensic training to Officers and staff. The incumbent is also responsible for document-ing crime scenes with photographs, video recordings, diagrams and reports.

Minimum Requirements: High school diploma or GED; supplemented by college level coursework with emphasis in Crime Scene Technology, Criminology, Criminal Justice or closely related field; Associate's or Bachelor's degree preferred. Four (4) years experience in crime scene processing and forensic science and criminal investigations, to include a minimum of one (1) year of supervisory experience. Completion of formal course in basic fingerprint identification, advanced latent fingerprint identification and administrative ad-vanced fingerprint identification conducted by the FBI preferred. Knowledge of computer forensics is highly desired. Experience with a wide range of computer hardware and soft-ware is preferred to assist in the collection of evidence from the various types of computer systems. This position requires effective verbal and written communication skills as well as the ability to interact with law enforcement personnel, city staff, general public, and at-torneys. Must possess and maintain, throughout employment, a valid Florida driver li-cense and satisfactory driving record. The position involves irregular shift work and shift rotations necessary to provide services 24 hours a day. Applicants qualifying for employ-ment will be subject to a polygraph examination and an extensive background screening.

Police Officer I, II, III (Certified)

Deadline: Open

Salary Hire-In Rates* Police Officer I—$46,002–$66,808 Police Officer II—$49,682–$72,152 Police Officer III—$53,657–$77,924

* Salary Hire-In rate will be determined based on years in Grade as an Officer and edu-cation attained. Actual offer will be determined by the City's Human Resources Depart-ment after a thorough review of an applicant's file.

Nature of Work: This is a highly responsible position with the City of Miami Gardens that involves networking with the community and the protection of life and property. This is accomplished through patrol work, criminal investigation, community policing, code enforcement responsibilities and enforcement of the laws of the State of Florida and the Ordinances of the City of Miami Gardens. Assignments may typically involve routine motor patrol, bicycle or foot patrol, or criminal investigations. Officers receive assign-ments and instructions from police officers of a higher rank and perform work in accor-dance with Department policies and standard operating procedures. Participates in special programs and projects as assigned. NOTE: The duties of this position will include all of those duties set forth in the official job description.

Minimum Requirements: These are the minimum requirements for the position. While the following requirements outline the minimum qualifications, the City reserves the right to select applicants for further consideration who demonstrate the best combination of knowledge, skill and abilities in relation to the needs of the City and the qualifications of other candidates. Meeting the minimum qualifications does not guarantee an invitation to test.

1. Be a United States citizen at time of application.
2. Be at least 19 years of age upon appointment.
3. Possess, or be eligible to obtain, a Florida driver's license and have an acceptable driving record.
4. Be of good moral character and never have been convicted of any felony or a misdemeanor involving perjury or false statement, or have received a dishonorable discharge from any of the Armed Forces of the United States. Any person who, after July 1, 1981, pleads guilty or nolo contendere to, or is found guilty of a felony, or of a misdemeanor involving perjury or a false statement, or domestic violence shall not be eligible for employment or appointment as an officer, in spite of suspension of sentence or withholding of adjudication.
5. Requires a high school diploma or General Equivalency Diploma (GED) equivalent (Police Officer I); or Associates degree (Police Officer II) or Bachelor's or Master's degree (Police Officer III) with major study in Criminal Justice Administration, Public Administration, Human Resources, Organizational Behavior, Psychology, or closely related field.
6. Proof of FDLE Certification or Police Officer Certification with training curriculum from home/state academy. Out of State Certified candidates must have one year of full-time certified work experience to be considered for the 92-hour Exam Qualification Course.

THE EXAMINATION/TESTING PROCESS is to determine if the "moral character" of the candidate is appropriate for employment as a Police Officer. "Moral character" is determined by examination of the life experiences of the candidate. Testing includes, but not limited to, the following listed factors.

EXAMINATION/TEST	WEIGHT OF TEST
Oral Interview	100%
Polygraph Examination	Qualifying
Psychological Examination	Qualifying
Background Investigation	Qualifying
Medical Examination (including drug screen)	Pass/Fail

Please deliver in person or send by US Mail (do not email or fax) the required documents . . . NOTE: all the applications, resumes, and requested material for this department go to the City's Human Resources Department.

Gresham, OR, Police Department

Entry level and lateral officers: $3,907-$5,255 per month

Lateral Officers credited one pay step for each year experience up to a Step 5 starting salary.

Apply online at http://greshamoregon.gov/city/

Call 503-618-2161 for more information

Located in the scenic Pacific Northwest, the City of Gresham is Oregon's fourth largest city. Gresham is just 15 miles east of Portland's city center, and less than an hour's drive to the Mt. Hood recreation area. Still a part of the Portland Metropolitan area, it is situated between the big-city hustle to the west and the solitude of the countryside to the east.

Specialties: Hostage Negotiation, Detectives. K-9, SWAT, Bomb Squad, Gang Enforcement, Organized Crime/Narcotics Unit, Neighborhood Crimes Team, Honor Guard, Child Abuse Team, Field Training, School Resource Officers, Training Instructors, Traffic/Motors, Hostage Negotiation.

DeKalb County, GA, Police Department

DeKalb County Police Department is leading the way with the highest pay in Metro Atlanta, Georgia and is NOW HIRING qualified applicants for the position of POLICE OFFICER

Starting Pay: *$36,504/year* with career progression to $62,856

Starting Pay with a College Degree: $38,328/year (4 year degree)

Advanced pay for Certified Officers with 2 years Experience: $38,700

Applicants must be 20 years of age, a U.S. citizen, possess a high school diploma or G.E.D., a valid driver's license, have no felony or domestic violence convictions and an honorable discharge if veteran. Officers certified in other states with a minimum of 2 years experience may qualify for an abbreviated academy and above entry pay.

Benefits include medical group insurance options, a pension plan, a deferred compensation plan, merit salary increases, opportunities for promotion, 10 paid holidays per year, and paid vacation and sick days increasing with longevity.

For More Information Call:

Background and Recruiting Unit at (770) *724-7445* or visit our web site at www .dekalbpolice.com

CONTRA COSTA, CA, COMMUNITY COLLEGE DISTRICT IS NOW HIRING POLICE SERVICES OFFICER—

Contra Costa Community College District—Martinez, CA: $4,330–$5,275/Mo.

To perform law enforcement and crime prevention work on the properties, grounds and facilities of the District; to control traffic flow and enforce State and local traffic regulations; to perform investigative work; and to maintain public safety. No experience required. Requires high school graduation or equivalent and ability to possess a valid California Driver's License at time of hire; completion of a California P.O.S.T. approved Basic Police Academy at time of hire or possession of a California P.O.S.T. Basic Certificate; completion of Academy and/or employment in a recognized law enforcement agency must have been within the last 3 years or recertification by P.O.S.T. Passing a California P.O.S.T. physical agility test and run may be required. Online applications only. Please visit our website at www.4cd.net and click on career opportunities for full details and to apply for this position.

CITRUS HEIGHTS, CA, POLICE DEPARTMENT
POLICE OFFICER
PROGRESSIVE DEPARTMENT
4 WEEK   MINI-SABBATICAL ANNUALLY

LATERAL—City of Citrus Heights; *Open and Continuous;* $55,277–$66,332 Base annual salary. Benefits for Patrol Officers: 100% City paid PERS (3% @ 50); unique 4-week mini-sabbatical paid annually in-lieu of paid holiday time. For more information, contact Sergeant at (916) 727-5577 or visit www~joinchpd.net. EOE (329)

PIEDMONT, CA, POLICE DEPARTMENT

is recruiting for a FIT police officer position. Salary: $5,282–6,373/mo. + educational incentive & excellent benefits, including PERS 3% @ 50 (contract is currently under review). Candidates MUST have satisfactorily completed a Calif. P.O.S.T. certified academy prior to the final hiring date. Patrol Officers currently work 12-hour shifts and perform a wide variety of peace officer duties. City application is required and can be obtained by calling 510-420-3037 or by visiting our website at www.ci.piedmont.ca.us. Deadline: 5pm on 10/31/08.

CAREER OPPORTUNITY

Mount Vernon Police Officer

MINORITIES AND WOMEN ARE

ENCOURAGED TO APPLY

EARN UP TO $77,000 PER YEAR

Date of Written Examination:

SATURDAY, NOVEMBER 15, 2008

Last Date For Filing Applications:

THURSDAY OCTOBER 8, 2008

BENEFITS: including health and dental insurance, paid vacation, sick and personal leave, 12 paid holidays.

REQUIREMENTS: Candidates must be at least 19 years old by date of exam. To be certified for appointment, candidates must possess a High School Diploma or Equivalency Diploma, U.S.A. Citizenship and valid N.Y.S. Driver's License.

RESIDENCY: Candidates must be legal residents of Westchester, Nassau, Putnam, Rockland or all 5 Boroughs for at least 3 months immediately preceding date of written exam and continuously until date of appointment. Preference in appointment will be given to successful candidates who have been legal residents of the City of Mount Vernon for at least 3 months immediately preceding the date of the written test. A CANDIDATE'S RESIDENCY WILL BE INVESTIGATED AND VER1FIED BEFORE APPOINTMENT.

HOW TO APPLY: Applications may be obtained at Civil Service, Room 103, Mount Vernon City Hall, between 9:00 a.m. and 4:00 p.m., Monday Through Friday: or at http: llcmvnylexporttsites/cmvny3/de-partmentslciv/empioyment.html; or at Mount Vernon Police Headquarters. Roosevelt Square No. Mount Vernon, NY. You may also receive applications by mail by sending a Self addressed stamped envelope to: Mount Vernon Civil Service Commission, Room 103, City Hall, Mount Vernon, NY, 10550. Veteran's credits should be claimed at time of filing application by presenting Military separation papers (DD-214). ALL APPLICATIONS MUST BE RETURNED TO THE CIVIL SERVICE OFFICE IN PERSON OR BY MAIL WITH A NON-REFUNDABLE $25.00 FILING FEE NO LATER THAN 4PM. ON OCTOBER 8, 2008.

There are a number of civilian job opportunities in policing for candidates who have obtained their two-year degree. Some are career positions, which means they are not specifically for those who want to become sworn officers. If you are considering working full- or part-time while you complete your education, these positions can not only help you support yourself and your dependents, but also help you learn first-hand about policing and possibly gain preference points should you decide to apply for a position as a sworn officer in the future.

Bernalillo County (Albuquerque, NM) Sheriff's Department

YOUTH PROGRAM OFFICER I

Salary: **$ 13.06** HOURLY + **5%** HAZARDOUS PAY

Position Summary: Under general supervision of a Program Manager and Youth Program Officer II, is responsible for providing direct supervision, care and treatment of residents who are in the custody of the Juvenile Detention Center.

Major Duties and Responsibilities Summary:

1. Maintain security, order and discipline to prevent disturbance, escapes and insure the safety of residents, staff and the community.

2. Process new residents, including strip searching and showering, issuance of clothing, and orientation to the rules and regulations of the Juvenile Detention Center.

3. Maintain a written log of behavioral incidents and observation of residents; is aware of residents' room assignments; and monitors residents' physical location at all times.

4. Evaluate, recommend and implement programs that include education of residents in daily living skills, social skills and work/study habits.

5. Counsel residents in group and individual sessions.

6. Provide oral and written reports on residents to supervisors regarding their progress and problems of residents under the custody of BCJEC and its managed programs.

7. Assign and monitor activities of residents; supervise residents in physical education and recreational activities.

8. Observe and search residents and inspect and search facility as needed.

9. Transport residents to court, hospitals or other facilities and service locations outside of the Juvenile Detention Center.

10. Physically restrain violent residents, and if necessary pursue resident on foot, in the case of escape attempts.

11. Initiate contacts with parents, legal guardians, Probation and Parole Officers and other agencies.

12. Assist in the intake process when assigned.

13. Intake assignment also includes handling the control center, answer the telephone, and responding to visitors, court and law enforcement officers and others with business at BCJDC.

The above information on this job description has been designed to indicate the general nature and level of work performed by employees within this classification. It is not designed to contain or be interpreted as a comprehensive inventory of all duties and responsibilities required of all employees assigned to this job.

Minimum Qualifications:

1. Associate's Degree in law enforcement, criminology, psychology or related field plus two (2) years related experience working with youth in the criminal justice field.

2. OR a combination of four (4) years post-secondary education and experience directly related to the above duties may be considered in lieu of the above stated education requirement.

3. Knowledge of the goals, practices and techniques of corrections.

4. Ability to learn and apply the State Juvenile Code and other relevant laws and regulations.

5. Ability to interact effectively and professionally with administration, subordinates, co-workers, residents and the general public.

6. Ability to express ideas clearly and concisely, in oral and written English.

7. Ability to maintain composure under stressful or threatening situations.

8. Ability to utilize computer information system and operate communication equipment

Screening and Compliance:

The offer of this Bernalillo County position requires compliance with the following:

1. Employee must successfully complete the post-offer employment medical examination and a background investigation.

2. Employee must undergo 120 initial hours of on-the-job training, including State Juvenile Code and "A Level" Restraint Training. Employee must maintain certification in these areas every six months.

3. Employee must have a valid New Mexico driver's license by date of employment and retain a valid New Mexico driver's license while employed in this position.

4. Employee must comply with Bernalillo County safety policy requirements.

Working Conditions:

1. Duties are performed primarily indoors (90%) with some outdoor work (10%).

2. Indoor duties are performed in a temperature-controlled environment. Outdoor duties typically involve transportation of residents and recreational activities with residents.

3. Work hazards or potential work hazards include a possibility of personal injury from violent residents or heavy exertion activities while restraining or pursuing residents.

4. Employee may be required to do shift work.

Equipment, Tools, and Materials:

1. Utilizes computers and communication equipment on a daily basis.

2. Utilizes recreational/sports equipment, facility keys, handcuffs and shackles on a frequent basis.

3. Worker handles fire extinguishers and oxygen equipment on an occasional basis.

4. Operates a County vehicle as necessary.

Requirements:

Languages: English (First language)

Career Level: Early Career (2+ yrs experience)

Minimum Education: Associate Degree

Travel Requirements: No Traveling

Preferences:

Job Status: Part Time Employee

Position Type: Corrections—Juvenile Specialist

Sector: Local/County

Appendix C

Law Enforcement Glossary

THIS APPENDIX contains common law enforcement terms that you should learn if you have chosen a career in this field.

arrest. An arrest occurs when any sworn officer deprives a person of his/her liberty by taking that person into custody to answer for an alleged criminal offense or a violation of a code or ordinance that the officer's jurisdiction is authorized to enforce. Most arrests are made by police officers, peace officers, troopers, or sheriff's deputies, but depending on the jurisdiction or circumstances, probation, parole, or court officers may be authorized to arrest all or certain categories of people.

auxiliary/reserve/part-time officer. Designations that refer to different types of officers in different areas of the United States; regardless of title, they are found in many police departments and sheriffs' offices but rarely in state police agencies. Depending on local usage, these officers may be volunteers or may be paid. They generally perform in uniform a certain number of hours per week or per month supplementing regular officers during certain times of the year, such as in resort communities when populations increase substantially, or for certain events including traffic control or work at fairs or civic or cultural events. In other jurisdictions they have the same duties as fully-sworn, full-time officers. Although candidates for these positions may not be interested in employment as full-time law enforcement officers, many are and in some jurisdictions this type of employment is viewed as a stepping-stone to attaining that, offered first to those who are Police Explorers or others involved in similar programs or those who are on the civil service eligibility list, awaiting being called for full-time police employment.

background investigation. A key element of the hiring process, a background investigation delves into a candidate's past life, including education, employment, military service if any, criminal history, credit and driving records, and past associations. A candidate must provide information which is verified by the hiring agency as part of the process of determining whether the candidate is suitable for law enforcement employment. Deliberate falsehoods are automatic grounds for a candidate to be dropped from further consideration for employment.

beat. The smallest geographical area that an individual officer is assigned to patrol. In large cities and in high-density jurisdictions (airports, large train stations, etc.) an officer will likely be assigned to walk the beat; in rural area or agencies that cover a large geographical area (state police, suburban agencies) an officer will most likely be assigned to patrol the beat from a vehicle.

bureaucracy. Any organization with a strictly defined hierarchy; a defined promotion policy generally based on written tests; a career path; reliance on rules and regulations; and a formal and impersonal style of management. Police agencies, regardless of size, are generally considered to be bureaucracies.

chain of command. Each person in the organization is supervised and reports to one person, generally one or two ranks above him or her. For example, a police officer reports to a sergeant in most agencies—sometimes to a lieutenant, but almost never to a captain. A lieutenant reports to a captain or higher rank, never to a sergeant or police officer, both of whom are lower in the chain of command than the lieutenant.

civil service system. A system of hiring and promoting employees that is designed to eliminate political influence, nepotism, and bias, generally involving a written examination of factual material, and sometimes combining interviews and other criteria as part of process in hiring or promoting personnel. Most municipal, county, and state police departments and most federal law enforcement agencies are covered by civil service regulations; many sheriffs' departments and some special jurisdiction police departments are not.

civilianization. Describes the hiring of non-sworn employees (civilians), often to fill positions that were once filled by sworn employees. Among these jobs have been answering non-emergency and emergency phones, dispatching beat officers, investigating traffic accidents and civil infractions, and media relations. In recent decades, civilians have been hired to provide computer services and web design, crime and crime scene analysis and technical services, and budget and financial expertise.

community policing. A philosophy of policing that gained public attention beginning in the 1970s that is based on police agencies developing close relationships with civilian populations and developing partnerships to work more closely with the community to develop solutions to persistent crime problems.

criminal justice system. A description used to encompass the police, the judicial system, and correctional facilities and to show their interrelatedness as elements of a system of justice. The police are viewed as the gatekeepers to the system because they make the initial contact with law-breakers, and through the arrest process determine who will enter into the system. The judicial system is the middle phase, where guilt or innocence is determined, and correctional institutions are viewed as the final phase because it is where punishment is carried out. A broader description may also include probation and parole as alternatives to correctional institutions.

crime (criminal offense). Legal definition of an act that the government (local, state, federal) has declared to be unlawful; a crime is defined by law (statute) and is prosecuted in a criminal proceeding.

crime scene/crime scene investigators. The location where evidence of a crime may exist; over the past decade, the emergence of television programs that feature crime scene investigators (often termed the CSI effect) has led the public to focus on crime scenes and evidence obtained at them in greater detail than in past decades. In most large city police departments, crime scene investigators are sworn police officers selected for the job on a number of criteria; in some police and investigative agencies those who collect and analyze certain types of evidence may be civilians hired specifically for these tasks.

crime-fighter style. A philosophy of policing that was particularly popular from the 1930s to the 1970s that focused almost solely on the police role in fighting crime rather than on providing community services; this is the police role that is paramount in most fictional portrayals of the police, which many police candidates incorrectly believe will form the largest portion of their job responsibilities.

deadly physical force. Physical force which, under the circumstances in which it is used, is readily capable of causing death or other serious physical injury. Police officers are among the few government employees who are authorized to use deadly force under certain circumstances that are governed by department policies and court decisions.

decoy operations. A non-uniformed (plainclothes) assignment during which officers are assigned to play the role of potential victims with the goal of attracting and catching a criminal. Decoy operations can be very dangerous because the decoy is often unarmed and carries no police identification; this results in the decoy being totally dependent on the backup team (officers observing and positioned to assist) should the criminal attack the decoy.

detective. Sometimes called an investigator. Generally an experienced police officer who is assigned to investigate serious crimes by following up on initial information obtained at the crime scene by the patrol officers. In many police agencies, detectives are selected and appointed based on their active arrest records while police officers or having worked in plainclothes assignments. In some agencies detective is a civil service rank for which police officers must take and pass a written test to be selected from a list; this is similar to the procedure of tests and lists for chain-of-command ranks. The position of detective is highly sought after because it means working out of uniform, provides more freedom than is provided to uniformed police officers, and carries prestige, enhanced by the media portrayal of what has come to be known as the detective mystique—a view that detective work is glamorous and dangerous and that only detectives ever arrest criminals accused of serious crimes (felonies).

discretion. Freedom to act on one's own and make decisions from a wide range of choices; although police officers, particularly in uniform, are expected to act according to their departments' rules and procedures, police work entails considerable discretion by officers because situations may develop or change in ways that cannot be anticipated. Policing is often singled out as a profession in which the most important discretionary decisions are made by the lowest ranking personnel; this view is based on the understanding that it is almost always the officer who arrives at the scene of an event who makes decisions in which more senior or higher-ranking personnel are not involved until after the fact.

domestic (or family) violence. Incidents of violence between spouses or partners or between family members. These calls are disliked by police officers because they are often unpredictable and may turn violent when family members had intended for the police to simply stop a situation without using force or making an arrest.

drug testing (or screening). Analysis of employees or applicants for use of illegal drugs or substances; most agencies screen candidates at the time of hiring and many have policies for random testing of officers or of testing after a vehicle accident, shooting, or any situation in which impairment may have influenced the event.

evidence. Anything that tends to prove or disprove an alleged act (crime) or fact or action pertaining to a crime. Direct evidence is generally defined as an eyewitness account, a confession, or a tangible link to the act; indirect (or circumstantial) evidence is the deductive process of inferring an unknown fact from a known or proven fact. Physical evidence is anything tangible that links a person to the act under investigation.

field training (field training officer). On-the-job training that generally occurs immediately after completion of the police academy when a new officer (in most departments referred to as a rookie) is assigned to work with an experience officer (the field training officer). Depending on the agency, this period may last a few weeks and may be informal. In some agencies, field training may continue up to a year and may be a formalized program during which rookies are assigned sequentially to a number of training officers and during which the trainers file formal reports on the rookies' performance of particular tasks. In some agencies with formal field training, failure of the rookie to be positively appraised by the training officer may result in termination during the probationary period.

foot patrol. The historical method of patrolling, particularly in large cities, that lost ground to patrolling in marked police cars in the 1930s. It reemerged in the 1960s as a way to combat disorder and gained additional attention in the 1970s and 1980s as a community policing technique that makes officers more visible and accessible to members of the community. New graduates of a police academy are often assigned to foot patrol as a way for them to gain experience interacting with the public.

incident report. The first recorded, official report prepared by an officer after responding to an event; some incident reports are not followed up but others may be referred to detectives or investigators assigned to learn more about the event (generally referred to as a follow-up investigation).

informant. A civilian who has access to information about a past or potential crime who brings this information to the police. One type of informant may be an individual who is not involved in a crime but has knowledge of it, and has no other involvement with the police. Another type may be an individual who has been involved in criminal activity and assists the police in investigations, often for considerations of leniency in his or her own case. Although many types of enforcement depend on informants (setting up stings to purchase narcotics or guns by police officers are two such areas), police prefer not to rely on the testimony of informants in court and to verify information from informants through independent sources.

in-service training. A general term used to describe training that occurs after a police officer graduates from the academy. It might occur on a regular basis or as needed to instruct officers in new techniques, policies, laws, and so on; in some states a number of hours of in-service training is mandated for officers to retain their commissions (legal status as officers empowered to make arrests).

job analysis. A scientific or quasi-scientific method to identify the tasks that police officers perform and the knowledge, skills, and abilities (often abbreviated as KSAs) required to perform those tasks. A job analysis is often performed by consultants who ride along with officers to observe their activities or ask officers to list the KSAs they believe they rely on to perform their jobs, as a means of validating the requirements for employment. Agencies rely on these studies to create tests for applicants that are able to withstand legal challenges because they are recognized as being job-related.

jurisdiction. The authority of a law enforcement agency to enforce particular laws in specific political and/or geographic boundaries. United States law enforcement is highly decentralized; no one law enforcement agency has total jurisdiction, which means that no single agency has the authority to enforce all laws in all places.

lateral transfer. A transfer from one police agency to another while retaining rank or seniority gained in the original agency; these transfers are rare in the United States, where it is traditional that officers begin their careers at the lowest rank in one agency and remain there for their entire careers. The inability to transfer laterally is one reason it is important for candidates to consider carefully the agencies to which they apply, since quitting one and joining another will often require the officer to begin as a rookie in the new agency.

mentor. A person who fills the role of teacher, model, motivator, or advisor, generally a more senior member of the agency who takes an interest in the career of a new officer. The importance of mentors has been debated in leadership literature, but it is generally agreed that new officers benefit from having a senior person to whom they can turn for advice.

misdemeanor. A class of criminal activity below a felony; although the exact definitions differ by state, this class of crime is generally punishable by a fine of from $1,000 to $5,000 depending on jurisdiction, and a maximum of up to one year in a county or city correctional facility rather than in a state prison.

moonlighting. The term used to describe police officers working a non-police job during their off-duty hours; in some parts of the country it implies the second job is in private security, but it may refer to any non-police work. Regardless of the type of work, many agencies control of the hours and types of jobs police officers may hold during their non-work hours.

omnipresence. A concept associated with patrol that suggests that the sight of a uniformed officer, visibly patrolling on foot, in motorized vehicles, or on bicycles or horses, who appears to be always present (the literal meaning of omnipresence) will deter criminals from committing crimes and reassure citizens of their safety.

order maintenance. Expands the police role to one beyond that of crime fighter by emphasizing that officers are assigned to keep the peace and provide social services, not only to prevent crimes.

ordinance/infraction/violation. Although not identical, each of these terms refers to the least serious category of offense, generally punishable by a small fine and/or no more than a few days in jail, if any. They may not permit the right to a trial because a conviction may not result in a permanent record.

physical agility test. The portion of the entrance requirements for most police agencies that requires an applicant to complete strength and endurance activities found through job analysis to be required to perform police tasks. Tests might include running a particular distance within a designated time or completing specific physical activities (possibly sit-ups or push-ups) within a designated time. To accommodate the entry of women and smaller applicants into policing in the 1970s, many physical agility tests were modified; in many agencies, applicants are permitted to show these competences at the end of academy training rather than prior to acceptance into the academy. Although physical agility requirements differ across types of agencies and even within geographic areas, as a general rule state police and some federal agencies place a higher priority on physical agility tests than do other types of agencies.

police subculture. A subculture is a combination of norms, values, goals, career patterns, lifestyles, and roles defining a group that are somewhat different from the combination of these things held by the larger society. Of the many professional subcultures that exist, sociologists have found the police subculture to be among the strongest; suggested reasons range from the belief that people who are similar are attracted to police work, to the structured style of training and operations, to the reliance on other officers that the job tasks engender, to the potential danger the occupation presents, and to the fear of being isolated from peers if officers to do not adhere to the subculture's norms, which are viewed as secretive and as separating officers from civilians.

police cynicism. Cynicism can be described as seeing the worst in situations or in people and the belief that events or actions that appear positive will soon become negative. Police cynicism has been identified by sociologists as a belief that there is no hope for society and that people will always behave badly; it has been suggested that because police are often faced with negative situations they are more cynical than other members of society.

Police Explorers. A structured career and educational program that grew out of the Boy Scouts of America for young men, but that now enrolls both men and women between the ages of 14 and 20 and allows them to explore policing through volunteer work experiences in police agencies. Some Explorer programs provide accelerated entry into a department and, for this reason, Explorers and similar internship or volunteer programs should be considered by young people interested in police careers.

polygraph (lie detector) test. A test that relies on a polygraph machine to determine whether the person being tested is telling the truth; the machine measures physiological responses (perspiration, pulse, etc.) to psychological stimuli (the questions). Although many people question the validity of these tests, some police agencies use them in the hiring process to verify the truthfulness of applicant's claims.

precinct/district/stationhouse. Depending on local area usage, terms may refer to the collection of beats within a given geographic area, or to the organizational substations of a law enforcement agency. Generally, not all officers report to headquarters but rather to a building located within the area they patrol, which houses that area's equipment and supervisory personnel.

private security. General term to describe the industry that provides uniformed or investigative functions by non-governmental agencies. Private security officers (sometimes called private police) are paid from private funds. They may work directly for a company (termed proprietary officers) or may work for an outside provider (termed contract officers). The number of private security personnel far exceeds the number of police personnel in the United States; in 2000, the Department of Justice estimated that 2 million people were employed in private security, compared to approximately 600,000 police officers. Opinion differs as to whether working in private security provides experience helpful to a police career or whether the duties and legal responsibilities are so dissimilar as to not be helpful.

probationary period. The period from when an officer begins the academy until a specified time when the officer becomes covered by civil service or other tenure regulations. During the probationary period (generally a period from six months to as long as two years, depending on local law or union contract) an officer may be fired without a hearing or without the protections afforded by civil service law. Common reasons for termination during this period include conduct on- or off-duty that does not meet the department' standards or may pertain to something in the candidate's background that was not uncovered prior to hiring or during academy training.

random patrol. The patrol tactic of having an officer walk or drive around a designated geographic area in what seems to the public to be a random manner but may be predetermined by patrol supervisors. The theory behind random patrol is that officers create a sense of omnipresence by appearing seemingly at any time; the tactic is based on the belief that the surprise presence of officers creates a fear of detection in criminals and therefore creates a sense of security in members of the public.

sting operations. A type of uncover operation where officers pose as something they are not to surprise and arrest criminals. In some cases the police may pose as criminals by setting up a store in which to purchase stolen goods, or they may pretend to be looking for someone to commit a crime for them. Other types of stings have used a different element of surprise; officers may invite criminals with warrants for arrest to, for example, a party or event, which they attend with no expectation of being arrested.

SWAT. Special Weapons and Tactics teams began in the 1960s. The term is used to describe teams of officers who are specially trained and equipped to deal with situations that present a higher-than-usual level of danger, such as hostage-taking situations, or situations in which it appears there are multiple aggressors. SWAT training varies across jurisdictions but generally ranges from hostage negotiation to special weapons training, including training as sharpshooters. In large agencies, SWAT members are permanently assigned to this team; in smaller agencies they are likely to maintain their regular assignments but are called for SWAT duty when a situation occurs in which their skills are determined to be appropriate. There has been criticism of SWAT teams in smaller agencies because there are often few situations for which their skills are required, leading to their use at times at which it is perceived as an overreaction to the event.

undercover operations or investigations. Covert (hidden) activity undertaken by police which during which officers work in plainclothes (out of uniformed, either in normal business attire or in clothing appropriate to the undercover situation). Officers attempting to observe the purchase of guns or narcotics, or pretending to be gun purchasers or drug dealers, would dress differently than officers posing as businessmen attempting to buy a restaurant to use as a front for money laundering. Undercover operations are seen as among the most dangerous in police work; officers must convince others that they are authentic in the roles they are portraying and must often work without their police identification and firearms, and in some undercover situations must position themselves to become crime victims while depending on a hidden backup team of officers to come to their aid as the situation develops.

Appendix D

Additional Resources

THIS APPENDIX contains a list of useful resources that will give you more specific advice on areas with which you may need help during your career planning and job search.

OTHER LEARNINGEXPRESS TITLES

Becoming a Border Patrol Agent. ISBN: 978-1-57685-681-9.
Border Patrol Exam, 4th ed. ISBN: 978-1-57685-575-1.
California Highway Patrol Officer Exam. ISBN: 978-1-57685-589-8.
California Police Officer Exam, 2nd ed. ISBN: 978-1-57685-588-1.
Corrections Officer Exam, 3rd ed. ISBN: 978-1-57685-652-9.
Court Officer Exam. ISBN: 978-1-57685-580-5.
Job Interviews That Get You Hired. ISBN: 978-1-57685-549-2.
Police Officer Exam, 3rd ed. ISBN: 978-1-57685-567-8.
Police Sergeant Exam, 2nd ed. ISBN: 978-1-57685-572-4.
Probation Officer/Parole Officer Exam. ISBN: 978-1-57685-582-9.
State Trooper Exam. ISBN: 978-1-57685-583-6.
Treasury Enforcement Agent Exam, 2nd ed. ISBN: 978-1-57685-537-9.

MAGAZINES, NEWSPAPERS, AND NEWSLETTERS

Although there are a number of regional police newspapers and newsletters, there are fewer national magazines than you might expect. However, subscriptions rates are low and most provide all or the majority of their content online.

If you are attending a college with a large police studies or criminal justice program, it is likely that the campus library subscribes to a number of national and regional police publications.

In addition to the publications listed in this section, many of the professional associations described in Appendix A publish monthly or quarterly magazines that can be accessed through the associations' websites. Some provide only highlights, but others, including the International Association of Chiefs of Police (IAC) *Police Chief*, are available complete in .pdf format from the current issue to many years past.

Publications that provide a realistic view of policing include:

American Police Beat

http://www.apbweb.com

This is a monthly newspaper written for police officers; stories are generally very pro-police and come from all around the nation. Many of the articles are written by police officers. Articles are easy to read and although some are quite opinionated, others are less emotional and more informative. There are a large number of ads placed by police departments with job vacancies. Most of the magazine's content is available online but the display ads of job notices are not.

FBI Law Enforcement Bulletin

http://www.fbi.gov/publications/leb/leb.htm

Published monthly by the FBI, this magazine is read by law enforcement professionals from all areas of policing. It is available free by mail but the entire contents of each issue going back to 1996 are available in .pdf format that can be read at the computer or easily downloaded.

Law and Order

http://www.hendonpub.com/publications/lawandorder

A monthly publication of Hendon Publishing Company, which publishes a number of specialized police magazines, this is a general magazine geared to police officers. Some opinion columns are written by police officers, but many of the articles are focused on more than one department and provide examples of what different agencies are doing to address current police issues. Subscriptions are available to the print magazine but the entire contents of each issue for a number of years are available in .pdf format that can be read at the computer or easily downloaded.

EDUCATION-RELATED SITES

These sites allow you to input information about yourself and search for colleges, internships, and the money to pay for them based on your preferences. You can also find guides to help you to determine those preferences.

Test Prep

www.learnatest.com

Offers effective online practice tests for law enforcement members and candidates with instant scoring and personalized analysis. You can also find career advice and test-taking tips.

Internships

www.internships.com

Contains general and regional guides for internship possibilities nationwide.

www.internjobs.com

Provides a national database of internships. Students and recent graduates can search the database by keyword or location and post online resumes for employers to view.

Scholarships

www.gripvision.org

A free online magazine, "written and edited entirely by teenagers," includes information and a search engine on scholarships, financial aid, grants, loans, and colleges.

www.scholarships.com

"The Largest and Fastest Free College Scholarship Search on the Internet" allows users to create a personalized profile comparing their scholarship needs to a database of over 600,000 college scholarships award programs.

Financial Aid

www.finaid.org

"The SmartStudent' Guide to Financial Aid" lists and explains eligibility for student loans, scholarships, military, and other types of programs

www.fedmoney.org

A comprehensive list of all U.S. Government programs benefiting students. It includes information on grants, loans, scholarships, fellowships, and traineeships.

ONLINE EDUCATION

Many colleges today cater to those seeking college degrees or certificate programs in a large number of police studies and criminal justice related fields. The programs listed here are a small sample of what is available. Each was chosen because it has connections to some of the professional associations described in Appendix A.

American Military University

http://www.amu.apus.edu

Despite its name, this all-online university is not solely for military personnel. It claims to have 30,000 enrolled students studying in over 100 countries. The university offers degree programs in criminal justice, legal studies, and homeland security. Webpages for each major provide details on course requirements and offerings. With physical headquarters in Charles Town, WV, and an administrative office in Manassas, VA, AMU is a member of the American Public University system (APUS) and is accredited by the Accrediting Commission of the Distance Education and Training Council (ACDETC), which is recognized by the U.S. Department of Education (DOE).

Columbia Southern University

http://www.columbiasouthern.edu

Specializes in two-year, four-year, and master's degrees in criminal justice and is accredited by the ACDETC. CSU is approved for use of veteran's educational benefits and, in partnership with the National Sheriff's Association (NSA), extends tuition discounts to NSA members, their spouses, and children.

Northcentral University

http://www.ncj.edu

NCU offers a number of degrees with specializations in criminal justice, homeland security, and public administration. Students are advised they need not visit the physical college in Prescott Valley, AZ, until their graduation. NCU has education partnerships with a number of law enforcement groups, including The FBI National Academy Associates, the Fraternal Order of Police (FOP), and the International Association of Women Police (IAWP). It is accredited by the DOE and the Council on Higher Education Accreditation (CHEA).

Federal Law Enforcement Training Center

http://www.fletc.gov

All but a handful of the federal law enforcement agencies conduct their basic and many advanced training programs at one of FLETC's locations. The newly designed website does not provide a link to the more than 60 federal law enforcement agencies trained by FLETC. However, going to the link titled Training leads to Programs and clicking on Basic Programs will provide a candidate with information on specific training programs of some agencies. The Employment link may be misleading as it is not a posting of jobs for the individual agencies; it is meant for those who seek employment directly at FLETC. Information on the College Intern program is available on the site (http://www.fletc.gov/student-information/college-intern-program) is open to students who are United States citizens enrolled in either a bachelor's or master's degree program and majoring in criminal justice, criminology, or a related field.

INDIVIDUAL DEPARTMENT OR AGENCY WEBSITES

One of the easiest ways to learn about a particular department you are interested in joining is to check whether the department has a website. Thousands of police and sheriff's departments have a presence on the web. Some sites are professionally created. Others are labors of love maintained voluntarily by an officer or group of officers. These sites are an excellent way to learn about a department. Some provide detailed information on hiring standards, including educational or physical agility standards that applicants must meet either to take the entry exam or at the time they are hired, and whether openings currently exist. Some agencies have pages addressed specifically to women applicants, who are often concerned about family-related issues and about meeting the physical agility requirements.

Many department sites have a link for interested applicants to send questions to be answered by a member of the department or the jurisdiction's personnel specialists. Even if this type of material is not available, an applicant can get a sense of the style and philosophy of a department merely by considering how it presents itself to the public: What types of police specialty units are featured? Are names, phone numbers, and e-mail addresses of key personnel made available in a way that indicates the public is encouraged to communicate with the department? This is an excellent way to get questions answered that you might feel are very elementary or that for any reason you do not want to ask in person.

Most recruiters are aware that applicants are sometimes concerned about feeling foolish; they will encourage you to ask any questions that are on your mind, but for some, the chance to do so with only an e-mail identity is comforting.

POLICE-RELATED COMMERCIAL WEBSITES

If you are unsure where you want to begin your career, many commercial websites provide links to applicant discussions, listings of agencies seeking applicants, and law enforcement news articles from around the country. They include:

Copseek

http://www.copseek.com

Although the homepage is quite busy, the site is easy to navigate; click on Directory on the upper left-hand side of the page for links to more than 1,000 U.S. police agencies, arranged by state. Police Jobs, another section, is in part password protected, but a few jobs were listed for all to view. The site also presents a roundup of police news stories and discussion forums.

Narcotics News

http://www.narcoticsnews.com

A section entitled State Page Resource Page allows an applicant to link directly to all state police agencies. The section opens attractively with three pages of patches representing each state's police or highway patrol. By clicking on the state, the candidate arrives at a page with further links to each state's drug assessment, list of officers killed in the line of duty (fallen officers), the state's sex offender registry, and, lastly, employment information. This is the direct link to the individual department's webpage. Most agencies provide detailed information on their hiring requirements, many concentrate on physical agility requirements (which tend to be more challenging in state agencies than in most municipal or sheriff's departments). There is also an e-mail and a regular mailing address for each agency and an indication of whether the agency is hiring and, if so, when and where testing is scheduled to take place.

Police Locator

http://www.policelocator.com

Although this site was incomplete when viewed, if it is completed it will be very useful for applicants. With a clean, easy to follow design, the entry page allows a visitor to click on the name of a state and be taken to a page decorated with the state flag followed by alphabetical links to police and sheriffs' departments within that state. The list was impressive for states that were completed, but as of fall 2008 many states were shown to be under construction; since the copyright date was listed as 2006, there is also a possibility that newly created departments will not be listed.

RealPolice

http://www.realpolice.net

This is a busy website but is easy to negotiate. There are sections that list jobs, all of which were current at the time the site was reviewed, and offers a feature where you can limit your search by ZIP Code, a section on police human resources, forums and chat areas, and useful hints on career issues and undertaking job searches.

Sameshield

http://www.sameshield.com

This website, devoted to historical and present issues involving women in policing, is maintained by a retired high-ranking female special agent. There are numerous photos and bios of early women in policing and current leaders in the field, as well as a section devoted to women killed in the line of duty. Potential police applicants, particularly women, should be interested in learning that women have been in policing for more than 100 years; there is also a frequently asked questions area, and library and resource sections that feature books on policing and links to numerous other websites, including a number of colleges with criminal justice programs.

Security on Campus, Inc.

http://www.securityoncampus.org/schools/policesites.html

This is gold mine for anyone interested in campus policing. The link, Campus Police & Security Web Sites, is exactly that, a 15-page list arranged alphabetically by state of all campus police departments within that state. Clicking on the name of any school takes the applicant in most cases directly to the campus police department's webpage, although some links are to the general campus site and require the visitor to locate the police department's pages. With a copyright date of 2008, it appears the site is maintained up-to-date. Campus policing has expanded greatly within the past decade; in addition to hiring many new officers, campuses have upgraded their security department into fully-sworn police departments and have begun to attract many college-educated applicants, particularly women and minority men, who expect to find the campus atmosphere to their liking and more likely to provide financial incentives for continuing their education.

The Police Officer's Internet Directory

http://www.Officer.com

After getting past the busy homepage of this site, someone seeking to learn more about policing or hoping to begin a police career will find a number of interesting items. In addition to a collection of national news items, there is a link to careers that provides links to departments that are hiring through a Browse All Jobs listing. There are also Career Forums that contain discussions on a variety of topics; other links are to law enforcement magazines, a listing of events, and a place to sign up for e-mail alerts on a number of police-related topics.

NOTES

NOTES

NOTES

NOTES

NOTES

NOTES

NOTES